MISSION, ANGUISH,
and DEFIANCE

MISSION, ANGUISH, and DEFIANCE

A Personal Experience of Black Clergy
Deployment in the Church of England

DAVID ISIORHO
Foreword by Anthony G. Reddie

WIPF & STOCK · Eugene, Oregon

MISSION, ANGUISH, AND DEFIANCE
A Personal Experience of Black Clergy Deployment in the Church Of
England

Wipf & Stock
An Imprint of Wipf and Stock Publishers
199 W. 8th Ave., Suite 3
Eugene, OR 97401

www.wipfandstock.com

PAPERBACK ISBN: 978-1-5326-7421-1
HARDCOVER ISBN: 978-1-5326-7422-8
EBOOK ISBN: 978-1-5326-7423-5

Manufactured in the U.S.A.   08/28/19

To my beloved wife, Linda who shared this journey of anguish and defiance. We were bloodied but not defeated. May God continue to bind us closely in our love of each other and of the divine presence. All in God's glad service. Amen.

CONTENTS

FOREWORD

My friend and colleague, the Revd. Dr. David Isiorho, has always remained a singularly committed and passionate individual whose adherence to a genuinely radical, authentic, and nonspiritualized form of Black theology in Britain has always been highly significant. I have known David for many years and his many articles in *Black Theology: An International Journal* and work on our editorial board has always been hugely impressive.

The provocative nature of this book is typically David Isiorho. David's firsthand account of his ministerial career in the Church of England is typically forthright and prophetic, which reminds us of the hypocritical nature of the church vis-à-vis her treatment of the prophets in her midst. The church has a curious habit of speaking in duplicitous tongues when it comes to those who ask penetrating questions and are challenging the institution from within. We will routinely read of Elijah, Jeremiah, Amos, Hosea, and John the Baptist in our lectionary, but rarely, if ever, correlate that with the embodied prophets in our midst who ask the difficult questions we would rather not hear.

In a former life, I remember David being omitted from any conversation about his suitability for a senior post at the Queen's Foundation because "Ministry Division" would not accept his appointment. The fact that a person with less qualifications, and who was White, was appointed is a critical reminder that the radical challenges David presents in this book are not solely in his imagination.

Historic mainline churches like the Church of England can be accused of adopting a neocolonial construct when it comes to appreciating the positionality of Black and minority-ethnic people within their ranks. I have witnessed the ways in which David, myself, and others who are deemed the "awkward squad" are marginalized in favor of lesser-qualified people who are positioned as more acceptable or perceived as the "good negroes" who will not rock the boat. I have argued repeatedly in a number of my books that how Black bodies are represented has not changed appreciably since the epoch of slavery and colonialism in this country. So, the Church of England, and other churches of its ilk, remains one that positions Black people within a narrow prism that exemplifies the worst excesses of respectability politics—the people who will show deferment to, and remain passive when in proximity to, White authority, with the latter remaining the only substantive posture expected by White authority in its relationship to structurally subservient Black bodies.

I am delighted to support David's book for the unflinching and searingly honest account of his ministerial career in the Church of England. This book should be essential reading for all people who want to see the emergence of a genuinely prophetic church that stands up for racial justice and will resist the toxic tentacles of White privilege and neocolonialism. I applaud David for his challenging insights and look forward to seeing the book in print.

Professor Anthony G. Reddie
Extraordinary Professor and Research Fellow
NRF 'A' Rated—Leading International Researcher
Editor
Black Theology: An International Journal

INTRODUCTION

HOW MANY CHURCH WARDENS does it take to change a light bulb? The answer is two: one to do the deed and the other to reminisce about the old bulb. A church that laughs at that has some self-aware people in it who realize that it is always time for change in this sublunary world. Sometimes, however, our churches need a different version of the joke: How many church wardens does it take to change a light bulb? None, because nothing changes around here. I have yet to work out the version that would suit the twenty-first-century green church; I could say none because they have solar power, but that might not really resonate.

This preamble was not without purpose as my methodology and delivery are key signifiers of my understanding of my own vocation as a priest and educator. Within that, as a lifelong learner myself, I am enthusiastic about theology and my rhetoric is under-girded by prayer. This book is about reaching out to my readers and meeting them at their point of inquiry to such an extent that I can wave them goodbye as they fly, informed and excited, into their own particular sunset. As a theologian and sociologist, I am passionate that people understand that theology is neither boring and nor does it have to be so abstract as to exclude the majority of inquirers. I use the term "inquirer" advisably, for inquiry and its close partner, reflection, should be at the heart of any Christian ministry. The long intellectual tradition of sociological investigation as a starting point for theological considerations has a strong pull for me personally. It is genuinely inspiring to see the sociology of religion active in our churches, helping us to take our Christian inheritance seriously, and transporting it to the twenty-first century.

I intend to use my own experience for the case study. I am an ordained priest of the Church of England, with nearly thirty years' experience in holy orders. I was brought up an Anglican, in the tradition of Anglo-Catholicism, although I now describe myself as a part of the Church of England, liberal, reformed, and catholic. It was not a smooth journey to ordination despite my early awareness that priesthood was my vocation. My Blackness posed difficulties.

It continues to present a challenge to the White institution of the Church of England. For example, I was the first Black vicar in a well-known, some would say infamous, Black area in the West Midlands, something that has taken quite some time for that church to achieve. Handsworth is an area of Birmingham which was notable for receiving a large succession of African-Caribbean immigrants during the Windrush era in the immediate post-war years. Handsworth is also a name associated with some so-called Black riots in the mid-eighties (actually, most of the violence occurred in a neighboring area, Lozells, but that is another story).

In my ministry and in my academic work, justice, compassion, and mercy are key. I cannot divorce my scholarly interests from my ministry as the one energizes the other in that very traditional Anglican way. At the heart of the Christian endeavor, I see the Christ who endured all we could do yet who remained in solidarity with us, never forsaking us, even to the cross and beyond. The Magnificat is the one piece of Scripture that I would cite as my mission statement. I am concerned for justice and rescue on both a large scale and at the individual level. This is backed up by the imperative to inform in order to empower. I feel strongly that worship has a role here and should offer people a variety of modes of discourse and expression that point their minds toward God, so the register and the spectacle are important. In other words, to comfort and to proclaim are the keynotes of my praxis.

I would describe myself as a priest who is aflame with the mission to bring wholeness into the everyday. I seek to bring to people a sense of their neediness before God and the assurance of their capabilities under God. For me, prayer and action cannot be separated so I seek to present the urgency for works of justice and witness that our Lord calls us to engage in to those who are in my care. As a Black priest, I am a living reminder to people of the realities of oppression and prejudice; particularly as a Black priest, I am a token of redemption and hope. We have a directive to bind, to include, for what God of love would ever want anything to be lost when it could be secured? I believe God gave us brains for a reason and that we should use them in rational, practical ways to change the world for the better. I therefore would describe myself both as an activist and as a meditative person who sees the here-and-now as an indicator of what is to come. In the Acts of the Apostles, Luke made it very clear that the kingdom depends upon the active participation of all with all the diverse talents and ministries this involves. Bringing people more deeply into faith should mean giving them more opportunities to minister in their own unique ways.

As an institution, the church can be explored as a context for race relations. The bishops I interviewed for this book described Black communities in the United Kingdom (UK) as flourishing, scattered, and vibrant, and some of these terms have unacknowledged pragmatics behind them. They emphasized the importance of forming ecumenical partnerships with independent Black churches and interfaith dialogues with other faith communities. Thus, with the help of the fund known as the Single Regeneration Budget, interagency work was encouraged to link the church with society at large at the civic level. The response of the Church of England towards Black communities was to foster multiculturalism, where we all learn about each other's customs within the safe confines of an apolitical and civic religion.

I have interviewed key people and quoted extracts in this book. In order to preserve the anonymity of the respondents, they are referred to as "RP" plus a number, (e.g., RP 39_. "RP" stands for Research Participant.

This city has been multifaith, multicultural, multiracial for decades. That is our future and we are committed to that and, as a church, my colours are firmly nailed to the mast. If they want to criticize me they can but my concern is for a multifaith, multicultural, and multiracial community in this city. There are people who complain that when people from other communities buy half the houses in the street and take over a whole area and compete with them for jobs then they become a threat. I think people who cannot see beyond that, who are inward looking and narrow minded will perceive their own well-being and way of life as threatened. The alternative is to see it as being enriched, which is my own particular view. If you look at England, we are mongrels. It is absolute rubbish to talk about the purity of the English. It is people who are threatened and are frightened or have some bizarre philosophy who move most easily into racism. What I am trying to do is to say that there are three stages broadly speaking. Firstly, get to know the person, don't put some label on them like Black or White. It tells you something, it does not tell you everything. Then see if you can do something together for the good of the community, maybe raising money on Remembrance Sunday. (RP39)

This bishop complained that criticism of his work with ethnic minority communities was an expression of the racism that still exist within White communities:

My suspicions would be that racism amongst White Christians is not difficult to find. But there is an increasing number who would be aware of it and do all they can to discourage it. I would be distressed to hear of a Black family in this diocese who were not made welcome. If I did have just a complaint, I would follow it up without delay. I don't recollect having one to date. I hear it said frequently that there has been discrimination, and people give themselves away occasionally with the odd remark. I certainly have received letters criticizing me for spending so much time with people of other faiths. "Why don't they go back home, bishop?" (RP39)

All research participants accepted that Black worshippers had been discriminated against in the fifties and sixties, and that racialized exclusion was still a possibility in many parish churches. This historical legacy was related to the formation of independent Black churches and there was general recognition that Black people still felt marginalized in the Church of England. Some research participants felt that racial awareness training would address the issue of racial prejudice, treating it as a product of poor education. Thus:

> The other thing as a bishop I think I should do is to promote racism awareness training and we have done this with the bishop's staff meeting spending two days at it. We have set up pilot projects in three deaneries and we are now ready to carry that forward. But there is quite a lot of resistance. People think that it's all about political correctness and that it meant to make them feel guilty. The way we experienced it when I did it was not like that at all. It made me do some heart searching. It was liberating. (RP36)

Racial awareness training offers us a sociopsychological view of racism which has been depoliticized. It is an individual response to what is largely an institutional problem. Racism is more than just a few misguided ideas contained within the psyche of White people. No amount of human relationship training by itself is going to change the working practices of institutions which work against Black people.

The race relations approach was related to a more general perspective about English society. Since most people could not be described as racist in any overt sense of that term, they could be reminded that to live in England had something to do with decency and fair play. The Church of England, having put its own house in order through organizational development techniques, could now establish its traditional role as a neutral party in community relations. Thus, the church could challenge racial disadvantage and exclusion in society at large by acting as a broker with and between other organizations in the pursuit of good race relations, and at the same time gain much need credibility in the urban context. The following extract from one of the bishops I interviewed gave focus to the role of the established church as a kind of broker between secular institutions and Black communities. The bishop comments thusly:

> I am chairman of a borough partnership board. They asked me to do it because they thought that, as a bishop, I would be a fairly neutral person. But this board is a group which comprises a lot of the agencies within the borough and is responsible for single regeneration budgets which support and develop work in the local schools and in the local colleges with Asian and Afro Caribbean groups. I am involved in that but that is a secular involvement rather than a Church one. I think that kind of involvement is worth doing. I think also the involvement through the racial equality council is well worth doing and I find myself sitting as a co-opted member on that council. Obviously, the concerns of the Afro Caribbean community there are very crucial. The monitoring of racial harassment and police involvement with Afro Caribbean groups has got to go on. And I am also the president of a One World group that works with all the different ethnic communities in the borough in a very creative way. (RP37)

Another bishop made the following observations:

> And I want to encourage lots of exchanges between different kinds of parishes. When I was vicar of a country parish in Bedfordshire, we developed a link with a Black Church in Bedford, a Black Pentecostal Church, . . . a half a dozen of us went to this Black Church for the evening and we got to know them through that and we said let's invite them over to a family service. And then I thought this is going to be awful and all the racism is going to come out, nobody will come to Church and it was going to be a big flop and people will be hurt. I didn't need to worry because more people came to Church that Sunday than we have never had apart from Christmas and special funerals. And people came out of their homes, they came out of the pubs. I suppose they had seen gospel singing

on the television and they came in large numbers. And the choir from the Black Church was very affirmed. And I sometimes think that perhaps we worry too much about racism. What we need is not to analyze our racism, that's something we need to do as well, but I am not suggesting we should sweep this under the carpet, but maybe we need more occasions in which people can share together as friends and share in worship and demonstrate that people are not racist in a terribly harmful way. There might still be a lot of things we have got to face. There is a great capacity for friendship and certainly the younger generation has far less prejudice than its elders. (RP36)

The following extract was in response to the question: What role do you feel the church can play in pursuit of racial justice, and within that context what can you as a bishop do?:

I think the church has to stand for friendship . . . But I don't think that negative campaigning is the most important thing that the church ought to be doing. This has to be done sometimes but I think it is far more important to build up trust and simply to make friends. There is the very human thing that people can simply enjoy each other's company and get to know each other and learn each other's stories. Jesus calls his disciples friends. And friendship seems to me one of the great gifts of the Christian gospel . . . And I think that spirit of open friendship and mutual curiosity, if I can call it that, is a very positive thing. Maybe what I ought to do is more entertaining of carefully chosen people. What we tend to do is to have a lot of clergy parties. We ought to do more to get people together to talk. Deliberately inviting people from different groups who wouldn't have met before. One of the things that the bishops have is a power of invitation. (RP36)

Another response is as follows:

Because we are the established church, the other faiths say, "We look to you, bishop, to be our spiritual leader in the sense that, because of your position, you must defend our right to exist and to practice our faith and our right to be free from discriminations." . . . Let me just mention one thing that I have found it difficult to know how to cope with and that is occasionally I am told that there is always unconscious racial prejudice. Now I don't know how to handle that because it means that I can never win. If I do something that somebody does not like, then I am excused of being unconsciously prejudicial. And I do know that as a human being I am motivated no doubt by all sorts of things deep down in my own psyche that I don't know much about. I am happy to admit all that. But I actually find it's more helpful to be encouraged by Black people and Black Christians to do better than to be told you are never going to win. I do believe in justice profoundly as reflecting the nature of God. And that must be applied in all walks of life. I have to live with the person that I am and in order to do better I need to be encouraged. I would never cast my vote for any party or candidate I thought was racist. I would never do so. I believe the future of Britain is to be multi-racial and multi-cultural and it is like a crucible. We are a small island with 56 million people. It is OK to put that number of people into Australia which is a heck of a size. But actually, if we get it right in Britain, we are offering something to the world that was far greater than anything which we offered in the Empire. It will be something for the healing of mankind. I have been ordained now for thirty-eight years. I have been in this diocese for five years. So, for the first thirty-four years of my ministry, I had never met a Muslim and I had not met many Black clergy either. My learning and growing up in that sense over the last five years, even at a ripe old age, has been astonishing. And, going to Pakistan for two weeks at the end of that five-year period, has shot the learning up yet again. And this is why I still come back alongside the structures to that personal thing because I was never hostile to Muslims, I was not very interested frankly in the sense that I had plenty of other things to do and get on with, but it is only when you have the meeting, because some of them are amongst my closest friends. So that process I think is quite important. (RP39)

What is clearly missing from this church race relations approach is a distinction between the concept of racism, which is about structural inequalities and racialism, which is about White prejudice. Without a clear commitment to sociological analysis on the part of the church, the concepts of racism and racialism are soon confused. Is the focus on the institutions and their institutionalized practices, or on the individuals and their individualized prejudices?

What follows is a critical review of John Wilkinson's work entitled *Church in Black and White: The Black Christian Tradition in Mainstream Churches in England: A White Response and Testimony*.[1] This is presented here as an example of the race relations ethos to be found in the Church of England. I use this work because of the importance of Wilkinson's work in leading ordinands; his influence, sadly, continues to this day. He was active around the time of my own ministerial formation, although I did not train under his aegis.

This book was apparently started in 1983 when Wilkinson hesitated before permitting a Nevis woman to sing a song at Mass the Sunday before her first visit home for over two decades. The woman sang "When I Travel":

> It is an old Sankey revival song, but sung by the two women, in harmony and without introduction or accompaniment, it is transformed by the sharp cutting edge of the Black tradition of worship. It has a self-evident power and spiritual authenticity and not a few members of the congregation are moved to tears.[2]

How else are affecting songs meant to be sung, one wonders? The normalization here of the anodyne English traditions of worship is astonishing and creates the first hurdle on the first page. Wilkinson then proceeds by writing three stories, beginning with his own, thus firmly setting a White frame, as in the title. My teeth are well on edge and this is only the second page! The second story

1. Wilkinson, *Church in Black and White.*
2. Wilkinson, *Church in Black and White*, 1.

will be about the Church of England, and then, last and thus least, the story of Black Christianity:

> The testimony is always self-consciously White; I have tried to avoid attempting to be a White voice for Black people.[3]

One wonders why the author did not therefore give the moneys raised for this project of writing this book under the supervision of James Cone, an eminent American Black theologian, to a Black person:

> If I, in telling my own story as a White priest of the Church of England, speak of "discovering" Black Christianity, I do so in order to testify to a spiritual journey—to testify indeed to a kind of second conversion. It is not that I discovered some new phenomenon, a strange sect in an obscure backwater, but that I found a new significance within the familiar. As a VSO teacher in the Caribbean country of Belize, I had already experienced how the history of the oppression of Blacks by Whites was still "live" history, still an issue needing to be worked through and resolved: the attentiveness and the "body language" of the children in class had changed markedly when we left the "dead" history of the Arawaks and Sir Francis Drake and turned to study the Slave Trade.[4]

This is arrant twaddle, so insufficiently worked through that Wilkinson cannot even have a specific set of terms but has to rely heavily on that refuge of the linguistically challenged, the inverted comma:

> Black Christian faith is rooted in an encounter with a new name, the "name above all names" which was hitherto unknown to Black people, the name of Jesus. Jesus, "de Lawd."[5]

---

3. Wilkinson, *Church in Black and White*, 3.
4. Wilkinson, *Church in Black and White*, 7.
5. Wilkinson, *Church in Black and White*, 13.

Why the phonetic? Presumably to add color?! This naiveté continues:

> The British Empire is now part of history.[6]

Lots of dry but detailed history now follows as Wilkinson tells those three stories. He quotes extensively and has clearly done his reading, albeit rather a long time before his date of publication in many instances. He cites, for exmaple, Michael Ramsay, who, in 1936, wrote:

> [The Anglican Church's] credentials are its incomplete-
> ness, with tension and travail in its soul. It is clumsy and
> untidy, it baffles neatness and logic. For it is sent not to
> commend itself as "the best type of Christianity" but
> by its very brokenness to point to the universal Church
> wherein all have died.[7]

Wilkinson quotes William Wolf, an American Episcopalian, who has suggested that Anglicanism is a:

> . . . pastorally and liturgically oriented dialogue between
> four partners: catholics, evangelicals, and the advocates
> of reason and experience.[8]

Wilkinson proposes this as his model for his examination of Anglicanism. Like Wolf, he sees the church engaged in a dynamic dialogue with the Spirit, leading to new and better futures. There ensues a passage of church history, interestingly, one in which Wilkinson places experience at the polar extreme to reason—a very White, Western, male dichotomy.

He concludes:

> If Anglicanism is a dialogue, the Anglican via media can-
> not be a static achievement.[9]

Of Anglicanism, he continues:

6. Wilkinson, *Church in Black and White*, 22.

7. Wilkinson, *Church in Black and White*, 91.

8. Wilkinson, *Church in Black and White*, 91.

9. Wilkinson, *Church in Black and White*, 93.

It has through centuries legitimated monarchy, empire, slavery and colonialism as well as class and ethnic loyalties within Britain.[10]

So, he is clear that Black participation within Anglicanism "changes the dialogue almost beyond recognition."[11] He then adds:

Black Christianity has a dialectical function which does not conduct dialogue in a discarnate, ecclesial sphere but brings explicitly into the dialogue the story of a relationship of oppressor and victim. Its task is first to negate; to lacerate the polluted core of Anglicanism, as the beginning of a process of transformation.[12]

This whole section is sharp and does present a person engaged in a struggle with history and circumstance. He relies heavily on American theologians such as Cone, which gives a profoundly un-English flavor to his thinking, which, in turn, limits any context for its application. He also appears to use the term "Anglicanism" to refer to the Church of England, which he does not depict as a cultural and theological reality distinct from the worldwide Anglican communion, the majority of which is Black. Since it was much to do with the Englishness of the Windrush travelers that urged them into the Church of England, and, since post-island thinking does not read like American thinking, one questions the relevance of this at the level of frame and of subdialogue.

He does quote the then-bishop of London, Graham Leonard, who wrote a letter to James Evans in 1983:

I think I should point out that there are no black Anglican churches as such in this Diocese. There are, of course, many churches with a preponderance of black congregations. The concept of black churches would be very difficult to fit with the role of the Anglican parish.[13]

---

10. Wilkinson, *Church in Black and White*, 94.

11. Wilkinson, *Church in Black and White*, 95.

12. Wilkinson, *Church in Black and White*, 96.

13. Wilkinson, *Church in Black and White*, 101.

Wilkinson goes on to outline features of Black Anglican worship that have a covert life on the periphery of the mainstream. Wilkinson introduces music, especially the slave songs of survival and liberation, in disjointed fashion:

> Some of the hymns, like Rock of Ages, Amazing Grace and some Spirituals, they sound more powerful. Those are the hymns associated with slavery. People would sing them every week if you let them.[14]

This seems an odd comment since these hymns have a strong and universal appeal that extends well beyond the boundaries of active worshippers of whatever origin. He seems to feel that Black singers have a special gift which can only betray a very narrow experience of other White cultures, to say the least.

Similarly, he feels that Black prayer is different from White free prayer. Of course, the role of free prayer within public worship varies across traditions, but nevertheless this does seem an extraordinary asseveration. Wilkinson also feels that Black preaching is full of feeling and fervor. It is a gift that one is born with, and is not something to be acquired through university education. Has he not heard, for example, of the White Welsh tradition of *hwyl* (there is no corresponding English term), the particular eloquence that an inspired speaker or preacher has?:

> But it should be noted that most group members found preaching the least satisfying aspect of the ministry of Anglican clergy.[15]

But that is by no means restricted to Black people. It may simply be a particular lack of ability on the part of the insipid White males that dominate the Church of England, or a reflection on the dominant discursive culture of the Church of England oratory.

Wilkinson's book continues with an irritating mixture of theories and dicta that are bound up against what can only be described as thoughts verging on biological theories of race, as above.

14. Wilkinson, *Church in Black and White*, 105.

15. Wilkinson, *Church in Black and White*, 109.

In essence, the book's problem is the colonializing of the field of struggle of others. It is not appropriate for a White person to apologize for Blackness. As one Black lay reader—indeed, at the time in 1989, the only Black reader in the Birmingham Diocese—remarked, it is always the nice Whites that get the funding to travel to the States to talk with Cone. It's great for them, but what does it actually say to the Blacks who are recognized and sympathized with, but yet are left in the struggle?

No doubt, Wilkinson means well, but I will leave the obvious aphorism as to the direction of well-intentioned journeys to the reader.

CHAPTER ONE

PARSON'S FREEHOLD

THE MATERIAL CONTAINED IN this chapter is ideographic. I use a case study methodology that is illuminating of processes, and although it is not proof of generic racism, it provides me with complementary data to support my accumulative arguments about English ethnicity. This report, as a case study, seeks to demonstrate the way in which my treatment at the hands of the church witnesses poorly to my community and circles of acquaintance. I feel that I have been forced into a position of challenge and implicit blame by the church which I regard as my spiritual home. This is a profoundly painful position to find myself in.

Whilst people in secular society now, after much training, easily raise the question of racism and racialization, the hierarchy of the church does not seem able to deal with real-life, right-in-front-of-me-now victims of racism. It is not that the church is actively involved in the process of propagating racism in any overt way. Its failures are more subtle, like the sins of omission. However, the church cannot rectify a failing it will not acknowledge. It is as if the vitality of sin operating within the human heart and at the center of the institution of the church simply cannot be acknowledged. Yet the suffering Lord that hangs before us is all about exactly that reality. The church compromises itself profoundly and seriously by its polite inability to see the issue for what it really is.

My credentials for this case study are as follows: I am a male priest, Black, British-born to a Black African father and a White English mother. I was thirty-two at the time of my deaconing. I had felt a vocation to the ordained ministry as a very young man, having always been involved in church life. I received no encouragement for a number of years; rather the reverse. I obtained a degree in sociology and became a social worker and Trades' Union activist. The persistent call to the priestly order continued however, and a decade later I was accepted and went into one of the older and more prestigious colleges to do my training.

I obtained, with comparative ease, a title post in the Midlands diocese which had sponsored me. During this time, I met and married a fellow ordinand, a White woman. This seems to have made a radical change to the way in which various diocesan officers treated us both. Their attitude changed from one of *bonhomie* to a stance of suspicion. I was given erroneous and potentially damaging advice about when to seek a move and was offered very little support by my diocese. A further example of racism, in brief, concerns the complete failure of my training vicar to grasp the vitriolic and clearly racist behavior of our neighbors. Canon Luke Wether's worldview did not include people who were willfully wicked, so he asked us to be nice to them. No priest should ever be that naïve.

When the time came to look for a first parish, I found that the circumstances in the church had changed fundamentally from the outlook predicted in my college days where I was assured that specialist positions would be the future for me. Posts were scarce and the competition fierce. During my title, I had gained a master's degree which made me a suitable candidate for chaplaincy posts in academic institutions. Usually I was not shortlisted on applications, and, again usually, would discover that the person appointed held fewer academic qualifications than I did and had less experience of academic life.

I came under some pressure from my training vicar who informed me that there was a precise time limit on my tenure. It became a matter of some urgency to secure another post. For a while, it looked as if I would have to accept another curacy which I was loath to do. Then, out of the blue, I received a communication from a Northern diocese inviting me to come and look at a vacancy in an inner-city parish.

From the beginning, the process seemed irregular. To this day, I have not clarified the legalities of my position there. The details of the first encounter will explain why I remained uncertain as to what it was I was being licensed to in this northern diocese.

The archdeacon wrote asking me to visit at such and such a time. In the letter, he named a neighboring priest as someone who would host the day since he himself would be away on holiday. It was also explained that the two parishes traditionally worked closely together. Nothing seemed to be strange up to this point.

On arrival, it transpired that this priest appeared to think that he was in the position of a team rector interviewing a prospective team vicar, not dealing with a colleague who was an equal. A Methodist laywoman, employed as a community worker, was referred to as a team vicar, which puzzled me greatly.

This priest asked some extraordinary questions. He wondered whether I was a man of God. He also queried about how I dealt with failure. Along with my wife, who had accompanied me, I had such grave concerns that we wrote to the bishop asking for clarification on lines of management.

It was also clear during the initial meeting that there was considerable tension between the two parishes, and that the host priest was uncomfortable and recognized there was conflict between the two parishes. The wardens of both parishes were in attendance and they indicated clearly that they each wanted their separate vicars. In fact, when this priest walked in as we were laughing together after lunch, he looked as if his face had been slapped. Everyone there noticed this.

I have a copy of the letter from the bishop commending me to these wardens which varies markedly from the letter of invitation I actually received from the archdeacon. Expressions such as "collaboration" and "informal team" are in the former but not in the latter.

A further meeting with the other priest was requested by the bishop. At this point, it was very clear from the papers that all sides had serious reservations. I obtained a copy of the letter sent by the other priest to the bishop in which he refers to me as the applicant in very disparaging terms. However, we both declared that we thought we could see our way forward after the second meeting. A unique license was drawn up in which we two were cross-licensed to each other's parishes as Honorary Assistant Curates in addition to the standard licenses. We were, therefore, clearly of the same status; me to assist him, he to assist me.

On my birthday, the licensing and cross-licensing took place, complete with cake, the hearty singing of "Happy Birthday," and a warden's enthusiastic invitation to give me a "right good Northern welcome." I laid my disquiet aside and looked forward to a new phase of my ministry.

It soon became clear that the early doubts were justified. The other priest proved to be very difficult to work with. The informality of the team was nonsensical. The two parishes were run as a team with the other priest very much in control. A team is a formal, contractual working arrangement bound by legalities. This priest would set agendas and organize meetings, usually at my house, in order, it later emerged, to ensure that I attended. This was entirely unnecessary since I have always tried to be a person of integrity and honor who would naturally attend meetings as expected. I have always thought my unhelpful colleague took himself far too seriously. In private, my wife and I called him Mr. Blobby, a well-known TV character characterized by a pink suit covered with yellow spots who would fall on the ground and have tantrums while waving his arms and legs. He appeared with Noel Edmonds on the celebrity's BBC television show, *Saturday Night Variety*. Mr. Blobby had a permanent toothy grin and jiggling eyes and spoke with an electronic voice.

My wife wrote a limerick.

There once was a vicar called Blobby

Who had team building as his hobby
He went about town
Got everyone down
Stopping them from doing their jobby.

So, the relationship with the other priest was not based on
parity of status. He would insist on sharing the morning office with
me at my church, never in his neighboring parish. He allowed his
newly ordained female deacon to treat me with rudeness. She apparently expected to be given a room in my house. (Later, her hus-
band was convicted of sexual offenses against a minor which she
must have known about as the offenses occurred in his vicarage,
their home.)

My wife, as will become clear, deals with crises by writing
poems, some of which are very sarcastic. This curate, Louise, had
been helping with English as a second language at a local Further
Education (FE) college. Linda wrote:

There once was a curate named Louise
With a smile like an infectious disease
She helped all de Blacks
Wid de tings that they lacks
She was ever so anxious to please.

A mediator, in the form of the bishop's Officer for Ministry
and Training, was brought in. This man from the cathedral was
clearly out of his depth and achieved nothing tangible. I can only
describe his input as ineffective and weak. Initially, he wanted to be
everybody's friend, but this did not help him find a way forward.
He wrote to me, complaining in the strongest tones that he was
unhappy with his role as consultant as this had now developed into
a passer of messages and receiver of complaints, although he was
still keen to assist in the process of direct communication between
the estranged parties. However, when he had clearly failed to bring
about any reconciliation, he walked away from this increasingly
difficult situation with his head held high.

So, what can we make of this? Was it just the case that he did
not understand the extent of the breakdown in communication or

appreciate why collaboration between the parishes and their clergy was deemed by the hierarchy as necessary in the first place? I think it would be fair to say that he also wanted to protect his future career and current position with the bishop. Unable to broker a meeting with all concerned, he leaves our story for the moment.

Meanwhile, matters came to a head one morning when workmen had arrived to do some urgent work to the roof of my vicarage. This delayed me from getting to my church to meet up with colleagues to say morning prayer. The other priest came out of the church and strode across to me. A glance would have told him what was happening but instead he ordered me to attend the office immediately in tones of considerable brusqueness. This, in public, was the last straw.

Meanwhile, my wardens had been pressuring me to go to the bishop and ask that the parish be completely independent. They returned from the meeting with the bishop to tell my wife that they had preferred me for the vacancy because they thought that I would stand up to this other priest. This is very interesting since they told the bishop's Officer for Training and Ministry that they wanted the collaboration to continue. Furthermore, they led him to believe that there was now a communication breakdown with me which was as great as the one between me and the other parish. I was glad when these two persons stepped down as church wardens and when others who were more appropriate and representative of the current congregation were elected to replace them. Over the years I have worked with a lot church wardens, but these people I inherited were the worst, lacking as they were in personal integrity. However, a lot would happen before the change of church wardens came into effect.

Suddenly, relations within the parish of St. Ewold's changed. Letters were sent to the bishop. Complaints were raised at every level. Hysterical and absurd accusations were flung around. For example, when I used the Third Eucharistic Prayer one day, certain members of the congregation thought that I was praying extempore and went into a tearful huddle in a side chapel. A letter of complaint was sent to the bishop who acknowledged his astonishment at their vehemence over such a normal exercise of priestly author-ity. Incidentally, the people had a full copy of the Order of Service and they had just to turn a page to find their place, a very Anglican way of worship. Another example was the attempt to provide cheap homemade wine for the mass when canon law is very clear about the quality of the wine to be used and about who is to provide it. The wine was completely undrinkable. My wife refused to taste it as she could smell its rankness from the other side of the vestry.

The situation degenerated with members of the staff of the neighboring parish insisting on continued attendance at meetings in my parish. They attempted to retain control over the finances. It seems fairly certain that some of their letters to the bishop and the archdeacon were written with the help of the staff of the neighbor-ing parish in a wholly unprofessional fashion.

A campaign began to oust me. When I queried about certain aspects of the finances of the parish, I was accused of innuendo and insult. The situation degenerated to near violence with a walk-out staged one morning and a picket line outside the church to prevent others from attending. Fists were shaken at my wife. I was called "the devil's disciple" for no concrete reason. Even the meetings of the Mothers' Union were used to stir up opposition toward me to such an extent that Mary Sumner House, the Mothers' Union Headquarters in London, intervened and disbanded that branch altogether. This did not stop the women from meeting in each oth-ers' houses, as we discovered one evening whilst walking the dog and spotted a cozy scene as the women crammed together in the erstwhile leader's house.

Numbers on the electoral roll stayed fairly steady but with a change of personnel. If the church community had been welcom-ing and outward looking, then they would have found that their new priest would have doubled the congregation. I know this from an analysis of service registers and other parish records. As it was, I replaced one set of worshippers with another, including some people who returned having previously been driven away by the vitriol of the most difficult of the parishioners.

A meeting of the parish was held chaired by the bishop's Officer for Ministry and Training. Yes, this man returns to our narrative, armed with promises from the bishop to make everything right. I listened to a litany of complaints against me from people who hadn't attended St. Ewold's recently but were clearly well rehearsed for this meeting. Because the other priest was not there, I declined to join in with accusations of my own. The bishop's officer promised that the bishop would find another piece of work for me and that the parish would have another new vicar. Neither came to pass.

The meeting was introduced by the bishop's officer, who began by outlining his own involvement, acting as a consultant in collaboration between the churches and on behalf of the bishop. In this capacity, he had met with all the clergy and had a detailed knowledge of the churches over the past few months. He continued by explaining that the bishop had asked him to convene this meeting with the congregation of St. Ewold's. This meeting followed on from discussions which had taken place between himself, the bishop, and the church wardens. I had a sense of much being done to me without me.

There was some disquiet expressed about the actions of the then-church wardens in that nobody had been aware of what had been happening until the previous weekend. The bishop's officer clarified that the church wardens had kept me informed of the meeting and that there was no reason to believe they had acted improperly or behind my back. We obviously had very different ideas as to what was going on. I decided to let this one go and not to challenge the chair as to the accuracy of the statement he was making. Clearly, some Parochial Council members were concerned that they had not been informed of events and so questioned the wisdom of the course taken and the lack of wider consultation.

The meeting continued, and the bishop's officer outlined the terms of my appointment to St. Ewold's against the background of an informal agreement of collaboration between the churches. He stated that there was some feeling that the terms of the appointment had not been as clearly expressed as they ought to have been.

He stated that the collaboration between St. Ewold's and the other church was not a formal arrangement, and that neither church had desired it to be formal and that the cross-licensing of the clergy at the two churches had been the result of this. He explained that, over the past few months, there had been increasing difficulties at the clergy level; there had been an exchange of letters between the clergy and that this had led to the termination of collaboration between them.

The bishop's officer emphasized that the bishop affirmed my courage in admitting that the collaboration was not working. However, problems arose because of the legal standing of cross-licensing and because it was understood from conversations with the church wardens that the congregation wished to continue the collaboration. Such continued collaboration would be inhibited if the clergy did not want it. The bishop's officer stated that since I had been appointed on the basis of the collaboration, if collaboration was not possible, it was perhaps right that I should leave. Some people felt that St. Ewold's would have difficulty in attracting a new priest and that it was fast developing a reputation of losing priests due to the lack of effective collaboration with the other parish. Clearly, I was not the first to find myself unable to collaborate with them at a clergy level.

The purpose of the meeting, we were told, was to explore how best to move forward from this point. Several parishioners expressed the view that they did not wish to start with the premise that Father David's leaving was a *fait accompli*. It was suggested that the experiment with collaboration had been forced onto St. Ewold's and, despite this situation, it was felt that the church had made the effort to make collaboration work. And, since it was not working, this may well be the time to terminate it. The view was expressed that the majority of parishioners had confidence in me as their vicar and in the growth of the church under my leadership. Some people felt that, given the circumstances, they would prefer to keep me as Priest-in-Charge and terminate the collaboration. Clearly this was not the view of everyone as the meeting was divided over the collaboration issue. A determined hardcore group of people wished the collaboration with the other parish to continue at any cost and felt hurt that I could not share this view. They had been worshipping at St. Ewold's for many years, this was the direction they wanted their church to continue in, and without the collaboration they could no longer feel that St. Ewold's was their church. A third group of people took the view that since collaboration seemed to be limited to social events, why did it have to involve the clergy anyway?

The meeting closed with the bishop's officer concluding that we had gone as far as we usefully could and that the most important thing was that, despite the differences, we could all continue to work and worship together. He took the view that there were strong feelings around and that the meeting had been important in allowing these to be openly expressed. He understood that no neat conclusions could be obtained from this situation and assured the meeting that nothing would be forced on me or St. Ewold's.

The bishop held numerous meetings with me, and each time would say something different until it was impossible to know what his mind actually was. First, he promised a living in "the White highlands," then he claimed that he had said no such thing. The upshot was I was given six months to get out.

This was enthusiastically reported in the local press with headlines plastered around the city. That was how my wife found out, driving back from work, and she reports that she had to stop her car to get out and vomit because she was so shocked. It was a visceral experience all around.

Thus, in due course, I received a letter from the Diocesan Secretary to this effect:

> I write further to the bishop's letter of 30th May 1995, acknowledged by your letter of 10th June 1995. As Secretary of the Diocesan Board of Finance, it falls to me to formally give you the three months' notice in writing, referred to in clause 4 of License, to determinate that License dated 18 August 1993 whereby you were permitted by the Board to occupy the premises known as Saint Ewold's vicarage. The Board hereby determinates the license on 30th November 1995 and you are required

to vacate the vicarage on that date. Please acknowledge receipt of this letter.

It could have been signed—a Christian.

This was less than halfway through a five-year contract. With the employment situation in the Church of England then parlous, there seemed very little chance of a future for me there.

So, my license to minister was about to be withdrawn. In all of this, I was not given the benefit of a hearing and representation. The circumstances that had led to the bishop's decision should have been reviewed. I was granted a license for a fixed term of five years, yet the bishop had decided to terminate this contract with three years remaining. At the time many people within and outside of the church could not believe that such a course of action was either desirable or wise. Reactions expressed to me were of horror at the bishop's apparent partiality. My wife and I were even stopped in the street by strangers, some of whom were members of other faiths, who expressed their concern and support for us.

The priest-in-charge of the other parish had a local reputation as an exceedingly unpleasant and difficult man. I was the last Black priest employed by this northern diocese which at the time did not escape public notice. I had the full support of my congregation in the stand I was taking. The Parochial Church Council, with new church wardens duly elected, wrote to the bishop informing him that at their meeting they had unanimously agreed that they wanted the cross-licensing arrangements with the neighboring parish to be ended. I had been asked to work within an inevitably conflict-laden, and ultimately inoperable, collaboration with a neighboring parish and its priest-in-charge. In this context, it now seemed to all involved at St. Ewold's that it was most unfair that I should now be facing dismissal. I had broken no laws either of God or of earth. Forgiveness and reward are available for certain favored persons currently occupying high offices in this church, which is entirely as it should be. However, in my case, I was left Father David, without a sling in a smooth place with no pebbles, facing a pitiless Goliath.

So, let us look at this rationally. What was the bishop's problem with me and my work at St. Ewold's? Why did he write to me saying that unless I voluntarily found myself another post within six months, he would withdraw my license? In common with most parish priests, I was required to live in accommodations provided by the church. Along with my wife, I faced the loss of our home for the past eighteen months, our ties to the local community, as well as a substantial part of our income.

The bishop gave three reasons for his decision. Firstly, he said that I refused to work with clergy from a neighboring parish. The truth is that St. Ewold's had now withdrawn from an informal agreement which it previously had given to the diocese to work with the other parish. It was a voluntary agreement. It did not work. The parish supported my withdrawal from the collaboration and my reasons for doing so. Secondly, the bishop wanted me gone from his diocese, because, as he claimed, I refused to reconcile with former parishioners. This is not true. I was subjected to vicious attacks by a small number of parishioners who, finding they had insufficient support in the parish, left the church. Threats and both verbal and physical intimidation were used against me, my wife, and other parishioners. Throughout this I tried to act with calm dignity. The individuals concerned have never sought reconciliation and have never shown any remorse for their own actions. Thirdly, the bishop implied that the financial position of the church was my fault. St. Ewold's, in common with many parishes, is very poor. It had a small congregation and was constantly struggling to meet its commitments. This had been the case for many years, long before I came on the scene. How could I be blamed for this?

So, what was the driving force behind the bishop's wrong-headed decisions? At the center of this was the archdeacon's personal dislike of me and his favoring of the other priest. Clearly, they both thought the latter was line managing me in a team situation, albeit an informal one. The archdeacon accused me of casting suspicion on the motives of the other priest and being discourteous toward him. Furthermore, he accused me of having a style of chairing meetings that others found threatening. Those of us who have studied racism sociologically are well aware of such trigger words applied too quickly by White people to Black people, "threatening" being a classic example.

In all disputes, the archdeacon took the side of the neighboring priest. On one occasion, I had to suspend a meeting of the Parochial Church Council, but not because the other priest was present, as was claimed by the archdeacon. I was fully aware that under the cross-licensing arrangements, he was allowed to be there. I adjourned the meeting because the other priest claimed the meeting was invalid as notice had not been duly given. However, the bishop's registrar and legal adviser gave support to me in following the local custom of leaving the paper work at the back of church for committee members to collect. The registrar was the only member of the bishop's staff team who ever showed me any respect. All the old congregation assumed that I was in the wrong and was operating some kind of campaign against the other priest.

I brought in my trade union to negotiate with the bishop, but to no avail, as he was not willing to change his mind and reverse the decision he had made.

News of my sacking was given to the press, without consultation with me, both by a member of my congregation and by the bishop. It really was a matter of faith as to whether or not my public ministry would be able to continue. I tried throughout to draw on my experience and skill as a trained psychologist and to leave open forums where people could express themselves without too much direction from me. It has been frequently astonishing, as well as bewildering, to have to deal with and understand the accusations and the lies that have been freely bandied around.

Upon reading the parish records, I find that St. Ewold's was used to this kind of atmosphere. Previous parish priests have experienced the same type of disputatious attacks. It is interesting that this time they were more vitriolic than ever. There are even documented accounts of former members of the congregation declaring that they wanted to have me removed. I leave it to readers as to why. I certainly have my own theories here.

Following the resignations, midterm, of the previous church wardens, arrangements had to be made to elect new ones. I would like to place on record my personal thanks to them for their care and stewardship of the parish at a time when their particular gifts were so needed. My thanks go to them also for their unswerving support of me as Priest-in-Charge of St. Ewold's. The new church wardens told the bishop in no uncertain terms where they stood. Father David was leaving St. Ewold's because he was dismissed from his post by the church hierarchy at the instigation of a small group of malcontents who had since left St. Ewold's. They told him they had to bow to the inevitable, but that did not mean they had lost sight of the unfair and racist manner in which I had been treated. The congregation would sing, for the last time, a hymn in solidarity with my situation, accompanied enthusiastically, as ever, by Linda on her African hand drum:

> Mother is a teacher, Father was a Chief,
> David is a preacher, but the bishop's given him grief.
> Crushed by the Goliath of Diocese and church,
> This poor little David has been left in the lurch.
> Bishop says he's got to go. The parish: we say No!
> For we love you, David, and we need you so.
> Both of the church wardens, all the PCC,
> On this central issue completely do agree,
> But the Nailsford bishop wasn't very kind,
> Didn't ask our views at all when he made up his mind.
> Bishop says he's got to go. The parish: we say No!
> For we love you, David, and we need you so.
> So, we charge you, bishop, you will not lose face.
> Reinstate our vicar, restore him to his place,
> Let him lead us forward in this community
> So that we can witness to our dear Lord's sovereignty.
> Bishop says he's got to go. The parish: we say No!
> For we love you, David, and we need you so.

The God of surprises came to my rescue. Eventually, I secured a seven-year contract in a Midland diocese in a parish within the Church of England's Catholic tradition. Even then, the long arm of Nailsford reached out to twist, as I was informed by a reliable source that there had been adverse telephone calls made.

My relations with the new parishioners were good and there was much mutual respect and affection. The allegations against me in my previous position, that I was violent and unduly aggressive, would have been met with the incredulity they deserve if they were to be repeated in my new parish.

My new parishioners talked about their vicar's gentle and perceptive personality and how this was much appreciated. My skills in negotiation and counselling, one of the reasons I was offered the position in the first place, were much used. I inherited a parish that was deeply wounded by my predecessor, who was in jail for serious sexual offenses against minors. I was tasked to commence the work of healing and comforting that was needed. No longer was I viewed as a man of no ideas who was threatening in his conduct. I felt trusted once more. However, I remained alert to any possibility of dissension and abnormally sensitive to any sign of tension. I continued with my PhD work, which had been my salvation and sanity during my time up north.

Because of that scary Nailsford experience, I did not feel entirely safe without the living, the freehold. In Gatesby Diocese, there was a policy of introducing fixed-term contracts when a vicar left, and a new person was appointed. The new vicar's job title would be Priest-in-Charge. I decided that I would apply for incumbencies with the living as they came along. Perhaps country living would enable me not just to broaden my experience of formal ministry, but also to foster my academic research and give me a chance to publish more regularly. I fondly anticipated a slower pace of life. How foolish this notion was!

Five years on from the relative safety of that West Midlands modern Catholic Church of England parish, I was lured into the delights of the East Midlands countryside and the formation of the Midshires group of seven churches ultimately.

Initially the benefice was made up of four parishes. During my first few months, I set myself the task of visiting everyone on the electoral roll. I had been to a number of social events in the various villages. I had attended the harvest suppers, the social evenings for new residents and the senior citizens' Christmas dinners; the Gilbert and Sullivan concert and the Christmas parties. I passed on the barn dance, but I enjoyed the fish & chip supper in January. I visited the sick at home and in hospital, as clergy do, and I worked with the benefice readers in taking communion to the house bound.

The idea was that each parish within the benefice would continue to have a rector, church wardens, and PCC. What clearly was impossible, and probably undesirable, was for the rector to be expected to administer each parish as in past times. It was therefore agreed to appoint a lay chair for each PCC, and that the day-to-day running of fabric, finance, and administration would not require the rector's direct attention. It was agreed that agendas should be published, circulated, and displayed in advance, and that minutes should be dealt with similarly after the meeting. Subsequently it was proposed that the rector would chair the Annual General Meetings and attend other meetings of the PCCs from time to time. It was also agreed that the rector would chair a benefice meeting with, say, two representatives of each parish and perhaps other particular organizations two or three times a year. The importance of the rector knowing what was going on without being overwhelmed was understood and agreed to by everyone.

At first, everything went according to plan. I sat in on PCC meetings and was pleased to see that everything was running smoothly. A few weeks into my new appointment, it was wonderful to see so many people from our PCCs at a social event at the rectory. I was beginning to get a sense of the whole benefice as well as of the individual churches.

The deanery had considered, consulted about, and decided upon a plan for the regrouping of a number of parishes some five years previously. My benefice was to be joined by three other parishes. So, we were now ready to consider the implications and to make plans. We met our friends from the other three parishes on a number of occasions and everyone had indicated their willingness to go ahead.

I convened three benefice meetings that year and they were very positive and forward-looking. The benefice meeting, or council, is made up of the church wardens, the benefice readers, the choir leader, and the Sunday school organizer. Our last meeting was held with the assistant bishop and archdeacon who explained that the timing of the enlargement of the benefice was reliant upon negotiations between me and a retiring rector who was only too pleased to hand over these parishes in September. It was not dependent on the arrival of additional staffing, such as a house for duty priest (a retired priest who usually agrees to work as a volunteer on Sundays and two other days a week in order to live in the parsonage house, and who does not receive any financial renumeration for this great privilege) who could provide much help in supporting me with my increased workload, however desirable that might be. I concluded at the time that this merger of parishes was realizable, but would require openness to God's will for all seven churches and for my ministry as their rector. I urged everyone to build on all the good work that had been done throughout the past as we entered this new phase in the life of our parishes together, seeking to make God's kingdom seen on earth.

On 2nd September, 2001, I was licensed as Priest-in-Charge of three more parishes. This second licensing meant that I became rector of seven churches working together as one benefice on an informal basis. I must have been mad. I was soon to learn that not everyone would be realistic about the rector's ministry or value what I was trying to do. I had left a one-church benefice where I was loved and respected to take on seven village churches where there emerged considerable opposition to my ministry. So, what went wrong?

There had been a settling-in period after my second licensing. I had been impressed with the overall attitude and approach of people to the amalgamation of these parishes. The rota of services was now up and running, and all the church wardens were supportive of the new venture. The newsletter was due to be amalgamated in the New Year and we had worked out a program whereby the choir could visit equitably and realistically across the seven churches. People were beginning to visit services across the benefice. We also had several people on a deanery-wide study program led by me and the rural dean. There was a lot of encouraging goodwill around, or at least I thought there was.

I reiterate the question: What went wrong? It all centered on whether I should be promoted from Priest-in-Charge to full incumbent rector, with freehold rights that would allow me to stay at the post until I was 70. Normally this would have gone through without any objections. When I left to return to urban ministry, the White person who followed me became the rector, area dean, and honorary canon of the cathedral without dissent. If only I had been White with county connections. It is interesting to note that my predecessor in that post was also accredited in the same way by the diocese. So why not me? Where was my preferment? What was the one clear difference between me and those other two colleagues? And, talking about this predecessor, he never took a day off and eventually collapsed at a funeral he was taking which led to his retirement. He moved two miles away and came back to every funeral that I took at Midshires and looked down his nose at me. Clearly, I was not doing things in a manner he approved of, but such a response was very unprofessional of him.

So, two years into this rural post, all seven churches came to a common mind in support of a pastoral scheme to create the new benefice with myself as the rector. A year later, during the last, formal consultations, three of the parishes changed their minds. They put themselves in opposition to the new benefice and to me as its first incumbent.

My right good East Midlands welcome had started. A church warden who happened to be a corporate lawyer questioned the wisdom of the parson's freehold even though at the time this was the normal legal framework in Stoneton Diocese. I seem to remember that our Lord had problems with lawyers. This had not been questioned before when rectors were White, but now that the priest was Black, everything changed and things were viewed very differently. Anyone looking at this from the outside would have to question the motivation of these people.

The argument went as follows. No one should be appointed for life, whatever their ability, and it would be folly to tie a group of seven churches to an incumbency for a further generation. Thus, the freehold was now an outdated concept in the minds of these people. Their conservatism had led them to the realization that the parson's freehold was simply unsustainable in today's environment. Even in one of the supportive parishes where I was well liked there had been a reluctance to commit to a longer-term perspective which the reestablishment of freehold would offer.

The church warden in the village where my rectory was located was far more direct in his opposition to me. The pastoral scheme that would unite all seven churches was described as an imposition on this village that would saddle them with a thoroughly unsatisfactory vicar for the next twenty-five years. I was accused of taking no part in the life of the village and of not knowing who my neighbors were or where they lived. According to this man who lived over the road from the rectory, no one in the village had a good word for me. I was further accused of not answering my phone on my day off and being seen in my dressing-gown at noon. This man was a judge and, yes, nobody in this village or anywhere else thought that they would get any justice in his court. The really scary thing was that he presided in the family court where so many bad decisions have been made historically.

When I eventually left the countryside and moved out of the rectory, I left behind that dressing-gown on the gate so that this obnoxious neighbor would see it. I also left behind a car that I was looking after for a priest friend who was working with the Mission to Seamen in the Netherlands. The car, not the dressing-gown, became the symbolic focus for further conflict or, at least, I think it was that way round.

It was now halfway through May and I had moved to a new parish. Abrupt and offensive letters started to follow me to my new urban location complaining about the abandoned car. I had spoken to the properties manager of the diocese about the car before I left in February. The idea was that it would remain at the rectory until the summer and this had been agreed upon. I asked my former neighbor to address all future correspondence concerning the vacated rectory to the properties committee and not to me as a former parish priest.

I wrote to my friend about the car explaining that I had two extremely unpleasant, threatening letters demanding that we have the car removed by some arbitrary deadline that my erstwhile neighbor had plucked out of the thin air with an unworded but very clear "or else" in the first letter. In the second letter this "or else" became "or else I shall inform your new bishop." Quite what the crime is in offering space for a brother priest to keep his car for a short while, well, that baffles me unless it was because, as is common with impoverished clergy, the car was rather less than elegant. Snootiness and sanctity are not good bedfellows.

When I received the first letter, at my wife's advice, I wrote to my former area bishop who did not reply for some days. I then spoke to him on the phone and he agreed that the judge was exceeding his authority as church warden. The bishop was quite clear that a church warden was not responsible for the benefice house. Then I received a letter from the Archdeacon, someone new to the post and presumably unaware of the background. Joined-up management is not conspicuous in the Church of England.

The previous, very supportive, archdeacon had been the one who spotted that the letters of opposition to me from this village had been typed on the same machine even though they purported to have come from different individuals. He also commented wryly on one occasion that the malcontents seem to have me under close surveillance. Letters had also been sent to the church commissioners and officials there sent a message via a friend to ask how my wife and I were coping. Their unofficial advice was to get out of there as quickly as possible. Even they, seasoned readers of diatribes, were appalled by the tenor and content of these letters. The deanery lay chair similarly could not understand what the opposition was based on for this vociferous minority. It does not take a great brain to figure out what would irk White people of this particular type.

The majority of people did not actually agree with what was a very personal attack on me, but very few were willing to stand up and be counted. However, a small number of people did have the courage to write to the archdeacon and tell a very different story about my ministry as they had experienced it. Two active members of the church community wrote to the diocesan bishop disassociating themselves from these letters, considering them to be ill-judged, breathtaking in their arrogance, and unrepresentative. These regular churchgoers found me to be sensitive, devout, learned, and approachable. A church warden from one of the supporting parishes wrote to the area bishop telling him I was sympathetic to their problems and worked conscientiously to further the gospel.

Getting back to the car, I still cannot see what the problem was, but my wife suggests that it reminds them that we were there in their precious village. If that was so, then their bile perhaps is explainable. In such a case, I would have expected the bishop and the archdeacon to have supported us.

We felt we had moved on. We are people freed by Christ from being stuck, from harboring venom. We just wished that these people would leave us alone. Their continuing invasion of our lives was upsetting, hurtful, and harmful, not least because it could well be a marker of their own inner states about which we both deeply prayed.

Bloodied but unbowed, I returned to urban ministry. I spent five years in the Diocese of Whitehead and then a similar time in Rougham. Both experiences were very positive, and I continued to serve under the conditions of freehold. However, I did encounter some difficulty with colleagues in Bootham in the first two years. My Black majority parish in Rougham came with a group ministry of White clergy who thought they knew what best was for me and how to manage me. Fortunately, I had some experience of this type of collaborative support and knew just how to deal with it. One instance is when preparing for a confirmation that would take place at St. Paul's, the colleagues actually gave me a copy of the liturgy booklet from previous years as if I had never organized a

Confirmation before. Its quality was poor, so my wife and I made sure that the orders of service we produced were to professional standards.

My brief story starts with the outbreak of war between my parish and the other three. A group youth club with the original name of Fusion had been meeting in my church. It was run and staffed by the other churches, whilst St. Paul's provided the venue. Following consultation with my church wardens, and after several attempts to get this group to follow the usual protocol of leaving a place as you found it, I had to ask this group to leave as they were making so much mess in the church room and piling up the furniture in the corridor. My elderly congregation found themselves putting back furniture and cleaning the room after every session to ensure the room could be used for fellowship after the midweek mass.

One of the church wardens, a Windrush generation, long-serving nurse, said she had been cleaning up "White shit" all her life and she was not going to do it anymore. The forcefulness of her expression meant that I could not pussyfoot around. My clergy colleagues believed my actions were disproportionate. The youth worker told me that it was my responsibility to get the room ready and presumably this included cleaning up afterwards. She clearly knew very little about churches as she referred to them as my "janitorial team." These people would not have talked to a White priest like that.[1]

The group chair, taking at least ten years off my life, told me that he thought I was in my early forties when I arrived in Rougham. Didn't they know "Black don't crack?" The truth of the matter is, I was far more experienced than most of my colleagues and more formally qualified, particularly when it came to practical qualifications as well as longer experience in formal ministry. They didn't like it.

There would seem to be a pattern of inner-city parishes with egomaniacs wanting to control the ministries of others: work with the poor to establish your cred and then move rapidly up

1. See Isiorho, "Tale of Two Cities," 195–211.

the preferment ladder, but whatever you do, do not empower the poor—just take charge. However, having the freehold really does make all the difference, as well as being blessed with an archdeacon who is a decent man.

I did not like these clergy colleagues from the start and I am sure the feeling was mutual. They seemed to have a model of ministry that had gone out with the ark. They thought that all decisions within their parishes should made by them as the clergy and decisions in my parish also by them as the White clergy. When I suggested that we should work in partnership with the laity and humbly recognize our ministry as the meeting point of many ministries, they clearly thought I had gone mad.

The clergy group met with the archdeacon in May 2010 to review the degree of collaborative working, in readiness for compiling documentation for recruiting a new priest to one of the parishes that was about to become vacant. The archdeacon reported to the meeting that he had met with the clergy on a one-to-one basis and was aware that they were finding the issue of collaboration extremely difficult and unsatisfying. An agreement between the clergy had been reached in August 2011 and was now seen as not working well.

At the meeting of incumbents/priests-in-charge on 3 August, 2011, it was agreed:

1. All four were committed to the continuation of the group ministry.

2. All would commit to meeting together (the "group chapter") not less than once per quarter, with other group clergy invited to attend and participate.

3. For these meetings, at least some specified group business would be signaled in advance, and forthcoming group activities planned.

4. Those group clergy who wished to meet more frequently for prayer and/or discussion would do so.

5. Dates for group events (e.g. Group services, confirmations, quiet days) would be agreed on with good notice, and individual churches would consciously aim to avoid arranging other activities which would clash. Furthermore, these events would be well publicized in each church, and the congregations encouraged to attend.

6. While it is desirable that all the chapter attend group services, it would not be taken amiss if this were not possible. There was no expectation that all clergy would necessarily be present at each group activity.

7. The deployment of the group curate was the responsibility of the training incumbent, who would judge to what extent the curate's involvement in the life and ministry of each church was helpful.

There had been a history of disagreements, different expectations of what the group should be and do, and also difficulties of communication about meetings. I was accused of being absent or late for group meetings even though colleagues failed to attend a scheduled meeting at my house. The current group apparatus was an unhelpful addition to the core tasks of parish ministry and my parish needed space to develop its own life. Whilst I enjoy collaborative working, I do not see the point in meeting for meeting's sake and not actually achieving any concrete outcomes.

However, I couldn't just walk out of this group and give them the satisfaction of being able to tell the archdeacon that I was the problem, not their racism. I had to box more cleverly than that. I knew what to expect, so I went to this meeting prepared and produced a statement charting the sequence of events, which was received but not discussed.

The group met in my absence in October. I had indicated that I would be coming from a school assembly, and likely to be later than 9:30 a.m. As it turned out, I did not get there until 10:10 a.m. and subsequently learned that the meeting had ended at 10 a.m. This was a very short meeting even for the Bootham clergy group, given that the agenda items listed in the group minutes included three group services. However, it was agreed by those present that the group chair would contact me about a date for the next meeting and I would be sent a copy of the notes. It was left to me to inquire about the next meeting scheduled to take place at my vicarage. Eventually, I received an email informing me that he and his colleagues were not willing to meet with me for the group meeting scheduled for 11th January.

So, what happened between October and January which led to this outcome? I can only surmise that my colleagues were unhappy that I was away at the end of October and not attending a group service at one of the churches. It was not unusual for clergy to go away during group events, in fact the quiet day only had the support of two of the incumbents. Furthermore, there was provision for this eventuality in the August agreement. What was their problem?

There are many common misconceptions of racism which can be very subtle. Post Macpherson's inquiry into the death of Stephen Lawrence, if someone involved sees racism then it must be considered. When colleagues chose not to attend the training day organized by the bishop's officer for Black and Asian ministries to facilitate consultation between White clergy and Black congregations, that was interpreted by me as having a racialized context, as I have recorded in my contribution to *Freedom is for Freeing*.[2] I do feel that it is unlikely that another White colleague would have been treated with what I perceive as the disdain handed out to me, as if I were some very junior priest still wet behind the ears. This group, historically, has been seen as White clergy supporting each other in a very Black place.

With regard to the overall health of the group, communication was very poor. I heard through the grapevine from my congregation that two colleagues were leaving; I was not informed separately nor treated as part of the group. Another example is that a confirmation date was changed without consultation or particular notice. Even if we had candidates in preparation, that would give little time for rescheduling.

2. See Barton, *Freedom is for Freeing*, 39–41.

By default, the group ministry disappeared. Not one of the group who used the excluding mantra of "we have always done it like this" was left. New incumbents have come, but nobody has wanted to reestablish a group ministry in Bootham.

So why don't they trust Black people? And by "they," I mean the White power structure that runs our church. The officials of the church must face their own racism. It is certainly more subtle than they likely realize. Racism is not to be defined exclusively as the activities of the extreme Right, which have nothing to do with the "nice" people who attend our churches. Nor is racism just about calling people names. Racism in the church is about institutions and structures and how they work against Black people: institutionalized racism, if you like. The racism we are talking about here involves institutionalized practices, not racial prejudice between individuals.

After twenty-four years in parish ministry and at the age of fifty-six, I started to take stock and to explore the possibility of making a further move before retirement. The post of canon professor at an eminent university was advertised toward the end of 2014. I noted that it was recognized that Black people were under-represented in academic posts in the university, and so applications from such minorities were particularly welcome. How patronizing can you get?

A crucial specification for this job was that applicants had to be Anglican priests. While there are certainly Black people in this country who could meet the academic requirements, I don't know how many Black people in holy orders who would fit the bill. I certainly would be a viable candidate! I have a PhD, but I have never had the opportunity to hold a full-time academic post and to build up the track record of publications and funding bids that this work would demand. Do not misunderstand me. I am pleased for people who feel that they are valued and preferred, but I can only cognetize one reason why, with the same or more qualifications, the same or more experience, I do not appear to be given the same chances. It is also about more than just preferment for me and even others. How do we open the church up, include all in the loving arms of Christ, if we so severely restrict the range of people who are in charge? For me, it is to do with richness in pastoral care, innovation in tackling structural issues that impede progress, and, burningly, it is about mission.

However, returning to reality, I saw an advert for an incumbency in the Church of Wales. It was presented as a dual-role ministry of a parish shared with a diocesan remit as a training officer for curates. As I read the job spec, my heart sank. It turned out that it was not a freehold position, but a Priest-in-Charge position under common tenure. The diocesan part was equivalent to one day a week. A sort of add-on, if you like. Furthermore, there were two worship centers, and these seemed to have the potential for some of the difficulties that I have described earlier in this chapter. Collaboration is the key word here. The parish had already started that long journey that leads to an amalgamation with three other parishes. All of this would lead to the formation of a ministry area that would facilitate a serious reduction in future staffing. In the meantime, as these parishes worked together more, who would actually be in charge? It was unlikely to be the newcomer. The church seems to specialize in fudging boundaries which usually results in a hurtful lack of clarity. I don't just do a job, I have a vocation which I am passionate about. So, do I see myself as being committed to working collaboratively across these parish boundaries? With my experience, the answer has to be no. This was a job with little security, or seniority for that matter, and was certainly not worth giving up a freehold for.

I then looked through *The Church Times* and a post as senior chaplain to a diocesan bishop caught my eye. It looked really interesting but, as I read the details, I soon discovered this senior job came with a get-out clause for the bishop and the diocese. The newly appointed officer would have to complete a probationary period of six months before the job could be confirmed as permanent, thus giving the bishop the right to terminate the employment of his senior aid with one month's written notice. So, we have here an interview and appointment system that is so uncertain as to its effectiveness that it requires such measures to protect the institution. Not to mention a bishop who doesn't seem to have confidence in his own powers of discernment when making senior appointments. Would I risk my employment and home on the good, or otherwise, judgment of a diocesan bishop? The answer had to be no. I had made some crazy decisions in the past, but this was not going to be one of them. In the words of the popular TV program *Dragon's Den*—"I'm out!

CHAPTER TWO

MISSION-SHAPED CHURCH

I HAVE CONSIDERABLE, DIVERSE parish ministry experience within the Church of England. I have been privileged to experience a range of parochial contexts in which to live and work, from inner city to rural-multiple-benefice. I feel this has given me a secure grounding in the types of challenges and hardships faced by the church as it seeks to meet the demands and aspirations of the communities we serve. So, in this context and in order to draw upon and extend that experience, I started applying for canon jobs in a number of cathedrals. There was a remarkable similarity between these appointments in that they all talked about mission and pastoral care. However, terms such as "equality" and "liberation of the marginalized" seem to be in short supply in the multifaceted and extensive world of cathedral ministry. Nevertheless, cathedral ministry combines peculiarity with particularity, a very specific contextualized mission.

So why did I want to become a cathedral canon and why did I think I could thrive in such an environment? And why did I think that the White men who run our church would entertain the idea of employing me at this level of seniority?

As the first Black vicar in a well-known Black area, my work was a marker of a deeply pastoral, healing, and consoling presence.

This has helped me understand what a ministry of being means through the way my presence has helped many people gain their own voices. I also feel this has completed a journey of enrichment for me that would allow me to operate on a bigger scale beyond the parish boundaries in the wider church and world. There are so few Black priests in senior posts in the Church of England that these applications were, in part, a challenge to that glass ceiling.

Was I punching above my weight? English cathedrals set the bar pretty low when they say that the person appointed needs to have been a priest for at least six years. The next bit of the person specification usually asks that the candidate demonstrate outstanding pastoral skills. It is amazing what successful candidates can cram into a short period of time. I filled in the application form and explained that I had been in holy orders for twenty-four years, along with a shorter period as a social worker, and that during that time I had gained experience in the provision of a wide range of pastoral care. Furthermore, I had professional qualifications in counselling and social group work as well postgraduate degrees. Cathedrals usually want staff who are confident preachers and are not put off by large gatherings. Well, if I was a shy, introverted type of person I would never have considered public ministry. So, yes, I like leading worship and especially at services that are well attended, which mine frequently are, especially with Afro-Caribbean funerals. I explained in my application that on two occasions I have preached in a cathedral setting, once to over 1,000 officers and cadets of the Air Training Corps at Titchfield Cathedral, and I even worked with the Dean of Armswell for a funeral service that we could not fully accommodate because of the number of mourners. For me, the aesthetics of worship are important. The music and rhythm of worship are signifiers of the divine and beauty betokens the spirit.

My own feeling about preaching is that this has changed over the years, particularly vis-à-vis modern media. A good sermon has to have a robust structure and be succinct. People will no longer sit to a discourse that occupies forty minutes. This is not a question of acceding to the sound bite, but of responding to the need to be clear, accessible, and memorable. Good preaching needs to use modern imagery and symbols as signposts to the deeper meaning of our faith and its continuing relevance. Our starting point is always that internal dialogue with the Holy Spirit, the undergirding of prayer without which ministry is a hollow sham.

Clearly cathedrals want people with a track record of leading churches into growth and they often talk about working closely with young people. In Lowshire, I was involved with initiatives that were known as *Fresh Expressions*, seeking to establish new or different forms of church for a changing culture. The new approach here was to extend our worship and play group of a dozen parents and children to become a group of sixty-plus. It was very much about drawing new people into mainstream church. By way of contrast, I was involved in a critical engagement with the insights and experience of the season of invitation as a successor to the Back to Church Sunday. I set up visiting teams to support an increasing number of housebound communicants. I believe a mission-shaped church is one heart speaking to another across the suffering of the human condition. It is the tiny movement of the Spirit in local places where the members of the church take others under their wing just as the Everlasting God has us all under his enduring wings. Thus our mission statement was that we seek to lead all to Christ by church contact with the wider community and see this as an important part of a much larger process of church growth. We are the people of faith, and it is in the faith of Christ Jesus that we continue this important work. I first used this statement when I was vicar of the Ascension and it was adopted by my then-bishop to use across the diocese.

I believe that at the heart of any ministry is pastoral care. The word *pastor* means one who feeds, the nourisher, the sustainer, ready to lead, to follow, to comfort or to afflict, to walk beside people during the barren days and to celebrate alongside during times of richness, to visit and care at all times. In practical terms, this means actually visiting people in their homes, their workplaces and leisure places, finding out what is important to them. If we don't visit them then we can't expect them to visit us (i.e., attend church). Visiting on a one-to-one basis gives a real demonstration of the importance of each individual and creates a spiritual intimacy that is affirming. This may seem old-fashioned, but this is how I do ministry. I also believe that this is a wider ministry than merely a priestly one. I always seek to develop teams of lay people who are ready to go into homes to meet with the people. We do need to be careful about how these lay ministers are recruited, trained, supported. For example, a clergy visit prior to a baptism for instruction is crucial, whereas any follow-up work may well be suitable for lay visitors otherwise the people may think that the church is populated solely by clergy. Within this, careful clergy will remember that it is sometimes the most active and apparently autonomous parishioners that may need the greatest and most delicate pastoral care themselves, thus mission and pastoral care combine.

Cathedrals talk a lot about support for volunteers. If I had been interviewed for a post as a cathedral canon, I would have had the opportunity to explain that ministry is all about empowering the laity to develop new skills and confidences, and seeking and nurturing specific vocations. Active members of the congregation are all volunteers. If we can't work with volunteers, everything will crumble. There is a real challenge in sustaining volunteers through encouragement, prayerful support, and attention to detail. Particularly as a Black priest, I understand what it is like to feel that you have no place or value. In one church, I engaged with the task of recruiting welcomers and greeters to support and supplement the existing team of sidespeople. It is not enough to give visitors to the church a hymn book and an order of service, it is actually important to take people physically to a seat and show them how the service will work.

I return to my earlier questions. Would I thrive in a close-knit cathedral community, living and working alongside colleagues? How would I fit in? My C.V. demonstrates that I am able to adjust well to change and am also able to function in a variety of settings. I am aware that tensions do arise within a collegial context, but I have the skills to seek to resolve conflict when it arises. I enjoy the positive interaction which exists between colleagues who live closely together and who pray together. In Lowshire, parish clergy were invited to do cathedral duty regularly, which I did. This has given me direct insight into something of the rhythm of cathedral life as well as the offering of pastoral care to casual as well as regular visitors.

The real question is this, "Do Black people work in such places?" The answer to that question is, "Rarely." I received those letters that start with the usual "Thank you for your application" and end with "I am sorry to tell you that you have not been included in those called for interview." There is often something about a "strong field" and that none of the applications were without merit, including mine. There is also a reassurance that all applications have been examined in some detail. "Thank you again and I am very sorry about the disappointing news." I wrote back to one cathedral and explained that I was not as disappointed as they thought since this was not the first time I had applied for a senior post and had learned to take rejection in stride, or words to that effect. The bishop was supposed to be away at the House of Lords, but he got in touch straight away when I sent an email asking for feedback and whether my ethnicity was a factor. As a Black priest, I wanted some clarity as to why I would not fit into the close community of his cathedral. The response was defensive and full of denial. The feedback amounted to a claim that I did not understand what the role of canon entailed and that my ethnicity played no part whatsoever in the decision-making process. Furthermore, they have been trying to increase the ethnic diversity of the clergy and were very nice to Black people. So what was my problem?

One of the cathedrals up north actually refused to consider my application on a technicality concerning ethnic monitoring. During a telephone conversation, I received some feedback. The observation was made that a ten-page personal statement was probably too long and required editing. However, this was not an issue that affected whether or not I should be called for interview. It was also pointed out that it was good that all aspects of the job spec/person spec had been addressed and that was to my credit.

The problem was I had not sent them my diversity form and this is what had ruled me out as a serious candidate. Furthermore, the word "Precentor" had been spelled incorrectly on more than one occasion and for a job requiring detail, there were doubts about my application. I pointed out that I was dyslexic and that such an observation could be potentially discriminatory on the part of the panel. I asked the dean if I had sent back my diversity form and corrected my spelling would I have been called for interview. He said it was difficult to say since my application had not been considered on account of the missing diversity form. Yes, I understand that bit but what if? Sometimes trying to have an intelligent conversation with a senior clergy person is like knitting fog. I subsequently checked my emails and found that his secretary had acknowledged my application and said she would get back to me if there was anything else they required. Why did they not tell me that the diversity form was not there? Fred, as we were now on first-name terms, eventually told me that an appointment had not been made and that previous applicants such as myself need not reapply. Goodbye—yours, a Christian.

The next section of this chapter considers the post ordination training of Anglican clergy, otherwise known as Continuing Ministerial Development (CMD), and my efforts to contribute to this field as a potential trainer.

My own CMD was not good. Sadly, my curate in Lowshire reported a similar disappointment nearly twenty years later. Part of my remit at The Ascension was to restore that church to being a training parish. I have aided three people through the process of discerning a priestly vocation and acted as advisor to others who were referred to me by diocesan training advisers.

I passionately believe that learning and professional development should be lifelong and ongoing. Part of our mission as ministers is to be ready to be as challenged as our people are by what life throws at us. To do this we need to be equipped critically and intellectually. CMD offers a precious opportunity for praxis to inform and direct theory and theology. You do not need to be clever to be a Christian, but your ordained clergy need to be up to speed. My academic interests revolve around mission, equality, and justice within a framework of pastoral and personal support for those I am working with. I have an interdisciplinary approach and move from the academic to the applied with gusto.

Key opportunities in equipping candidates for new patterns of formal ministry within today's church can be identified within the concept of lifelong learning. I outline this approach as set out in the Hind Report. A learning church is one that "promotes a dynamic and reflective discipleship for all its members."[1] It is within this context of the education of the whole people of God that candidates for new patterns of ministry are to receive their formation.

The traditional pattern of clergy training as a distinctive task requiring an exclusive residential formation dates from the late nineteenth century. The report outlines the perspectives from which this pattern is now under question. Clearly, the diversification of training offered by theological colleges is now beyond the traditional base of a residential setting. So, does the notion of shared ministry practically show in shared training without losing the distinctive elements necessary for both ordained and lay ministry? Candidates for new patterns of ministry within today's church can expect to move flexibly between gathered and dispersed settings, and accept this as a crucible for their theology of context as they grow in terms of service, holiness, vocation, and mission. They enter a dynamic and creative process of on-the-job training. Thus ministerial formation takes place in church settings, college campuses, and beyond.

Many of the challenges in equipping students for new patterns of formal ministry concern financial considerations. These in turn can be related to the flexible management of utilizing resources to provide high-quality and cost-effective training. We can outline some of the issues associated with the funding of candidates for formal ministry by examining the key drivers of costs. The Hind Report list numbers of these but the key areas include the following:

---

1. General Synod of the Church of England, *HIND Report on Theological Education*, 36.

- The number of people in training
- The ratio of staff to candidates in diverse modes of training
- The impact of information communications technology (ICT) upon effective training
- Income from property owned by trusts on behalf of the colleges
- Central church funding, which does not include fabric refurbishment
- Flexible pathways for candidates combining part-time and full-time modes
- Arrangements with institutions of higher education which bring in much-needed public funding
- Regional training partnerships, which share administrative services and academic staff.[2]

The challenge is to equip ministers for ministry within today's church, which should be bearing its witness in the world and to the world in a context of rapid change. Thus, training is there to equip the church to witness more effectively by serving God in the world. However, the pattern of training or equipping must be cost-effective and appropriate to the pastoral needs of today's church and its apostolic mission focus. These new patterns require wise stewardship of the church's resources.

Another question that needs to be addressed by both the Anglican and Methodist churches is the training of nonstipendiary ministers and those who train in a nonresidential setting, and then to relate this to our current context within the terms of the Hind Report. The church needs ministers but cannot pay them. The old style of ensconced clergy, secure in their parishes, supported by family patronage, indulging in their private gentlemanly hobbies of research, is long gone. The imperative is that the church, in one form or another, remains as the vital body of Christ on earth. That

2. General Synod of the Church of England, *HIND Report on Theological Education*, 89.

remaining must be undergirded by the tradition in the church of an intellectually and philosophically robust mode of teaching and development. The church needs to be realistic; the children of this world are wise in their generation. But, crucially, the church also needs to set its children free to do their own particular ministry, those good works that they each alone are called to do.

Is nonstipendiary ministry and licensed lay ministry being pursued due to financial constraints alone, or are we now beginning to recover a New Testament model where each believer brings and uses their gifts for the greater good and in due order? We are a rich church in that many of the people exploring formal ministry come with their own degrees and their own leaderships developed within secular fields. Can the church cope with all of this? Challenging people are not always easy to manage. Their abilities and life experience call for gentle but clear and informed managing and pasturing. My wife is a self-supporting minister, and, from her experience, I know personally that the value of the interface with society that this kind of ministry brings is incalculable. I also know that people in the world can all too easily feel cut off from the church and excluded. Managing their energy and including them in our daily lives can be difficult, and hurt people can subsequently become incapacitated. The other side of this is that clergy from a professional past can often feel distanced from that base and disempowered within their full-time stipendiary role.

The church today has to balance on a tightrope between reaching out and turning inward—growth and consolidation—always remembering that each of us is fragile and all need nurturing. Within this, the tradition has to be passed on and inherited, and reason has to be applied. Refreshing study is key to both processes. The imperative is that the church, in one form or another, remains as the vital body of Christ on earth.

Who am I to sit in judgment? Surely, those charged with these responsibilities know best? As a Black vicar who has worked in a parish with a congregation whose roots span three continents, I believe I can model a valid methodology of how to continue education that makes mission relevant to people. I think that through my clearly expressed commitment to lifelong learning, I can evince how clergy can be made more effective and more spiritual through real CMD that touches each person concerned and engages them. And what about the future? Angela Tilby makes the point that an aptitude for mission is now a criterion for discerning vocation.[3] Future ministers, like churches, are required to be mission shaped and willing to engage with fresh expressions.

So, what are fresh expressions? The term was first used in the Church of England report *Mission Shaped Church*[4] to give a name to a mission initiative which would establish new or different forms of church for a changing culture. The *fresh* bit of this term comes from a sentence in the preface to the Declaration of Assent made by Anglican clergy at their ordination, namely, to *proclaim afresh* the Christian faith in their own generation. It is an interesting play on words designed, presumably, to encourage not just the clergy, but the whole people of God, to engage with, and make their own contribution to, God's work in the world, with its clear reference to past, present, and future. Fresh expressions is part of Archbishop Rowan Williams's vision to create a mixed-economy church of traditional congregations alongside new approaches, and has the full support of the Methodist Conference. According to Steven Croft, this new way of being church and doing mission is well established, and is accepted as a way of keeping pace not just with the changes in, but also with the diversity of, British society.[5] The idea of a mixed-economy church is to go to where people are with the view of getting alongside new communities of faith by joining in with what God is doing in their context.

Fresh expressions is about doing things differently in order to realize the Christian mission, and as such it defies a real definition. A certain ambiguity is intentional and allows a substantial investment in the idea of resourcing a future generation of Christian adherents. For Croft, the key phrases of mission are service, incarnational mission, making disciples, and contextualization

3. Tilby, "What Questions Does Catholic Ecclesiology?," 87.
4. The Archbishops' Council, *Mission-Shaped Church*, 73–74.
5. Croft, "Fresh Expressions in a Mixed Economy," 1.

of the gospel.[6] The language of mission-shaped church and fresh expressions is provisional and inspirational in character. It provides a description for groups of people on a journey who are in the process of become a new community of Christian believers. However, there would seem to be a hierarchy about these developments. At the bottom are projects which are often high profile, with a least one full- or part-time member of staff operating under a bishop's mission order. The next stage up is something that is driven by a team of clergy and active lay people. This is likely to be an additional congregation to the benefice in which it operates. Further on still are projects that were envisaged as a bridge between what would be considered mainstream church services and events but which are now recognized as church activities in their own right. And finally, we have existing church communities that have undergone transformation and redirection so that their focus is clearly mission rather than maintenance.

For Lynda Barley, the Christian church in England and Wales bears its witness in a context of ever-greater diversity.[7] The ecclesiastical questions presented here focus upon a local context coming to terms with an external world which was probably not on its radar until the millennium. So, can fresh expressions help us get the gospel across as we manage this diversity or complication in the world order? According to Barley, the local *contextual mission* has to take into account changing patterns of church attendance and the possibility that the UK is undergoing a spiritual transition from older forms of communal worship to less formal structures of contemplation.[8] The idea here is that the church has to play catch-up and join in with these changes or be left outside to manage the decline. But, if organized religion is contextualized to the marketplace and churches are obliged to put on worship events designed to get the attention of the unchurched, can they do this without seriously compromising their commitment to the Christian faith?[9]

6. Croft, "Fresh Expressions in a Mixed Economy," 1.

7. Barley, "Can Fresh Expressions?," 161.

8. Barley, "Can Fresh Expressions?," 161.

9. Barley, "Can Fresh Expressions?," 164.

These are the big questions that the fresh expressions agenda seeks to address as it guides churches in their efforts to find socially relevant ways of being the church. A recurring theme in this literature is to show fresh expressions as representing not just a renewed interest in Christianity, but an increase in church attendance as well, particularly in the Anglican and Methodist denominations. For Barley, fresh expressions do precisely this—making a difference in terms of numbers and, as such, the potential to revive the fortunes of the Church of England.[10]

As a practical theology, fresh expressions is a catch-all term including forms of church which it is claimed to complement, contradict, and even supersede. As a method of doing mission, fresh expressions embraces alternative worship communities, café churches, and youth congregations that may or may not be about drawing new people into mainstream church. It also involves, for want of a better term, traditional church plants where new groups are formed as well as replants where old churches are reopened. Fresh expressions have been an important meeting place for the Anglican and Methodist church allowing these distant siblings to collaborate outside of the established frameworks. Fresh expressions is not constrained by the existing arrangements about ordained ministers, church buildings or public worship. Fresh expressions in this context is ecumenical and the only criterion of legitimacy is whether they are consistent with gospel values.

Alternative worship communities dating from the 1980s are often postdenominational and can be criticized for being weak on social engagement and lacking a clear mission focus. Another expression with similarities but very clear differences is base ecclesial communities whose origin is Latin American, and which enjoys the support of the poor and the marginalized. However, in offering a gospel of liberation for existing members, the emphasis is not upon mission and renewal.

A very popular fresh expression is the café church. The café ambience contrasts with church settings where a few of the faithful can meet the unchurched with a view to gently introducing

10. Barley, "Can Fresh Expressions?," 170.

them to something that may be loosely related to formal church. Thus, tables replace pews, often in a secular venue such as a school or youth club. Advocates would claim that this is in keeping with our Lord's table fellowship and have, in some places, introduced simple forms of worship.

Cell churches are a fresh expression that favors the small group. It is claimed to be effective where there are no strong family or community structures offering people a full-on, seven-days-a-week commitment where every member is expected to be involved in ministry and inducted accordingly. A cell church is not just small groups of people meeting in one another's houses, but rather a network of small groups that goes beyond the locality. Cell churches can be vague about sacraments and the ordination of ministers.

Martyn Atkins rightly locates the fresh expression debate within the context of Western churches and, in doing so, raises questions about what it is we call church and how it could relate to a fresh expression of its authentic self. The *hot questions*, as he puts it, concern the recognition of a fresh expression as either something loosely connected to church or linked in definite continuity with church. He comments that some people will accept a church meeting in a pub, while others would question the concept of pub-church, and others still would not be able to conceptualize the idea of a cyberchurch, if such a thing existed.[11]

For Atkins, the church is called by God to be the church in partnership with the blessed Trinity. Thus, the church has derived its nature from the Christian Godhead, which means the missionary task maybe with the church, but the initiative comes from God.[12] So the church's mission is God's mission. Thus, Atkins turns to the Bible to find the essence of church in God's nature and purpose where the New Testament missional perspective is the kingdom. Within this schema, God is seen as self-sent in the incarnate person of Jesus Christ to do God's will through resurrection

---

11. Atkins, "What is the Essence of Church?," 16–17.
12. Atkins, "What is the Essence of Church?," 17.

glory.[13] As the early church was established, it became a product of that mission as God continued to take the initiative through the Holy Spirit.[14] This is interesting, but where is the Pauline teaching or the theology of John in all this? It is as if the church was created to have no ideas of its own and that God imposed his cosmic desires and designs on it as an impression on smooth wax. Just at the point when it looks as if any notion of partnership with the divine is lost and a parallel might be drawn with a church run exclusively by priests and pastors, we are told to think of the relationship between God's mission and God's church as symbiotic.[15] Thus the missionary church has been called to be in partnership with a missionary God. Atkins tells us that this way of looking at church is implicitly contextual and that it is part of a natural process for other expressions of its essence to come forth.[16]

Atkins offers us three explanations as to the rise of fresh expressions in what he understands to be a post-Christian, post-Christendom era.[17] There is here an implied idea that the concept of fresh expressions had been identified and defined during Christendom. Thus comparisons can now be made about this during the modern and postmodern Christendom eras. Firstly, the church has always found fresh or new ways of expressing itself. Secondly, fresh expressions are associated with crises and conflicts which can be followed by renewals of faith and different ways of being the church. Thirdly, fresh expressions can be identified with either the church adapting to the existing culture or acting as a counter culture. Both these approaches will involve change and different expressions of what it means to be a church.

For Atkins, fresh expressions of church come into being when the existing structures fail to do their job. The missionary God calls us then to struggle with a new set of ways of being the church. This new expression of church is described as a new essence of church,

---

13. Atkins, "What is the Essence of Church?," 18.
14. Atkins, "What is the Essence of Church?," 18.
15. Atkins, "What is the Essence of Church?," 19.
16. Atkins, "What is the Essence of Church?," 22.
17. Atkins, "What is the Essence of Church?," 23.

whatever that means.[18] The problem with such an approach is that expressions and essences become difficult to identify and connote different things to different people. Clearly there is a political process going on here which means that the hot questions concern who has the power to make decisions about resources. It could be argued that a declining church is a fresh expression and that the faithful few remaining should learn the biblical discipline of the lament found in the Old Testament book of Ezekiel and the plight of the Babylonian exiles. This might be a better strategy for White majority churches that are not yet ready to embrace larger, multiethnic congregations and Black leadership.

Angela Tilby considers fresh expressions in terms of their catholicity and apostolic status. She identifies the church as crucially engaged with the historical Jesus whose postresurrection ministry is carried out through the mission of the apostles. The church's mission in the world is part of a continuous process of grace which one generation passes on to the next. Thus Jesus, sent by God, sent out the apostles who were to become the first bishops of the church, and they, in turn, through the laying on of hands, sent out others.[19] For Tilby, the church is God's mission in the world working through history, but it is not just a vehicle or means to that end. The church is that part of the world that is being transformed by grace and as such is a significant participant in God's wider mission to the world.

Tilby makes the point that advocates of fresh expressions from an Anglican perspective often appeal to history and to the Chicago-Lambeth Quadrilateral, which is premised upon a relationship between church tradition, the Bible, the Prayer Book, and reason. In the context of fresh expressions, the idea is to promote a flexible understanding of structures while maintaining some continuity with the past.[20]

An important critical evaluation of fresh expressions and the mission-shaped church agenda has been provided by Andrew

18. Atkins, "What is the Essence of Church?," 24.

19. Tilby, "What Questions Does Catholic Ecclesiology?," 78–79.

20. Tilby, "What Questions Does Catholic Ecclesiology?," 80.

Davison and Alison Milbank. [21] For these researchers, fresh expressions are defined as extraparochial interest groups that function independently from the parish structure of the Church of England. In stark contrast to the fresh expressions literature which advocates a consumer-driven approach to choice-led worship rather than Anglican liturgy, these writers seek to reestablish the relevance of the ministry and mission of the parish church as the inherited tradition. Furthermore, fresh expressions has abandoned Anglican ecclesiology in favor of the autonomous Christian,[22] Free Church Protestantism,[23] and the idolatry of mission.[24]

According to Davison and Milbank, the Church of England is currently experiencing a crisis of faith in that its informed membership lack confidence not just in the parish system and its Anglican heritage, but in the concept of the church and its place in the divine order of things.[25] They note the lack of theology and ecclesiological understanding in fresh expressions literature and assume, in one way or another, that church members have now accepted this alternative way of doing something loosely related to church.[26] They also draw attention to the contradictory signals given by the church hierarchy to promote common worship and, at the same time, give permission for all kinds of innovation and gimmicks to replace Anglican liturgy.[27] Added to this is the idea that what approximates to the Christian faith has somehow been watered down by fresh expressions in order to make it accessible to communities who are not in a good position to draw upon the resources of the parish church.[28]

So, what is the mission of fresh expressions? What is the goal? The conclusion reached by Davison and Milbank is that the fresh

21. Davison and Milbank, *For the Parish*.
22. Davison and Milbank, *For the Parish*, 58.
23. Davison and Milbank, *For the Parish*, 41.
24. Davison and Milbank, *For the Parish*, 54.
25. Davison and Milbank, *For the Parish*, 226.
26. Davison and Milbank, *For the Parish*, 225.
27. Davison and Milbank, *For the Parish*, 227.
28. Davison and Milbank, *For the Parish*, 231.

expressions movement does not know where it is going, only that they are not going to take the church with them.[29] If in the past formal church was a means to an end then, in a so-called post-Christian world, other and more effective means could be found.

For fresh expressions, the church is not to be confused with the kingdom of God since the former is earthly and the latter divine.[30] Thus the church is pushed to the sidelines even as a means to salvation. So, while fresh expression advocates may reluctantly accept the church as a signpost, it is the kingdom that really matters. Davison and Milbank note that, although John Hull[31] is a critic of fresh expressions, he too takes up this position.[32] Thus we are presented with a false dichotomy between either a mission-shaped church or a church-shaped mission. [33] An alternative way of looking at this would be to premise everything on the church as an agent of God's love in the world and make mission the dependent category. Thus, the church is not there to service mission, but rather mission is there to facilitate the church.[34] To reiterate the argument of Davison and Milbank, the church has an important role to play as an active agent in the salvation process, and she cannot be separated from her mission as some means to an end. Thus, means and ends are found in Christ as both the initiator and goal of our salvation. Agents and objectives are all one in the body of Christ, where the church is both beneficiary and provider of all good things.[35]

Fresh expressions also includes things that would not be considered different or experimental, such as Eucharistic services for midweek congregations, the use of *The Book of Common Prayer,* and family services on Sundays to accommodate multiple congregations. One of the fresh expressions described by the Church

29. Davison and Milbank, *For the Parish*, 54.
30. Davison and Milbank, *For the Parish*, 50.
31. Hull, *Mission-shaped Church.*
32. Davison and Milbank, *For the Parish*, 51.
33. Hull, "Mission-shaped and Kingdom Focused?," 114.
34. Davison and Milbank, *For the Parish*, 55.
35. Davison and Milbank, *For the Parish*, 60–61.

of England report *Mission Shaped Church* is traditional forms of worship.[36] This is presented as one of the most fascinating and challenging of the diverse ways that church is being expressed. An increase in attendance for those churches and cathedrals offering traditional liturgies has been reported.[37] There is a recognition here that people are seeking out the numinous. Traditional expression has been welcomed alongside new and innovative forms of worship, and the existence of the former is used to demonstrate the diversity that is on offer as well as to justify the latter. There seems to be no discussion here as to what the church's position should be if traditional expressions became so traditional that some of these congregations willfully seek to exclude marginalized groups. That would, of course, not be a fresh expression, but a perpetuation of the marginalization of Black people as down the ages.

We need a critical engagement with the insights and experience of Black theology in order to find out if there are any implications here for fresh expressions, or indeed any real connection at all. Certainly, it seems to me that there should be some dialogue ongoing despite the lack of contact or enquiry from the White establishment. I wonder how many people like me have been asked to participate in the consultation process of the next round of fresh expression initiatives when I was invited to discuss these issues with the research unit of the church army. The Church of England and the Methodist church of Great Britain are now committed to being the churches shaped for mission, but does this help them to fight racism and other forms of oppression? There is nothing in the teaching of Jesus to suggest that we can choose how seriously we take injustice. The gospel is not there to make us feel safe and comfortable. We have no choice but to commit ourselves fully to challenge what we know to be wrong in ourselves and the society we inhabit. And that commitment will put us into opposition with most of the values of this world, that is, in opposition to what Jacqueline Grant understands to be the three-dimensional

---

36. Archbishops' Council, *Mission-shaped Church*, 73–74.

37. Archbishops' Council, *Mission-shaped Church*, 73.

oppression of racism, sexism, and classism.[38] If it does not, then I would suggest we have the gospel completely wrong.

The next section of this chapter returns to the idea of lifelong learning (LLL) as a way of sharing my experiences of applying for ministerial training posts in several dioceses. I have always regarded this discipline as a godly one and have sought to (and succeeded) reach the highest formal degree standard possible. Since completing my PhD, I have continued my research and the application of my studies. My clearly expressed commitment to LLL demonstrates that I see how clergy can be made more effective and more spiritual through real CMD that touches and engages each person concerned.

I feel it is crucial for a Christian, and especially for a priest, to be able to engage with people of all ecclesiologies. So long as someone recognizes the name of Jesus, I can do dialogue with them, learning from them, and hopefully enriching their understanding of the faith and their own personal mission. For example, I was instrumental in setting up a multidenominational group in Lowshire called Shalom. I have led study days and parish retreats as well as my more formal educational enterprises.

CMD should entail primarily prayer. Prayer is a loving discourse that ensures the Holy Spirit is central to human interaction. Following that, the people in CMD courses should be nurtured and enabled in their ministries. This involves careful and individual interactions with CMD providers to understand where each clergy person is at and what their needs are.

I have applied for several posts as a continuing ministerial education officer. I usually start my application by informing a would-be employer that I am very self-motivated, and that part of my sense of vocation is the drive to find out what I can develop within myself to bring to the Lord's service. The parable of the talents springs to mind. Whilst I am very ready to work outside office hours, I am also very practical about time management and ensure I am just as refueled through downtime as I am by throwing myself wholeheartedly into my work. My equally busy wife and I make

---

38. Grant, *White Women's Christ*, 209.

sure we have time together on a regular basis. We both draw much strength, comfort, and challenge from this.

In my applications to become a CMD officer, I go on to say that I see the possibility of this post as one that will draw together much of my experience to date and make use of it in a holistic and focused fashion. I am ready for new tasks and different ways of working and of pastoring. At a practical level, the Church of England must empower more people to be able to exercise a ministry, as in the early church. We have perhaps allowed too narrow and too institutionalized a model of ministry to become the norm. For the reinvigoration of faith at the grassroots level, all vocations need to be identified and acknowledged, fostered, and nurtured. I also say that my commitment to equality of opportunity comes from my strong sense of justice. As a Black priest in the Church of England, I live out a model of equality that I use gently to foster dialogue as necessary. My preferred scriptural expression of this would be to say I am a Magnificat Christian. Having said all of this, I am yet to be invited to interview in response to an application as CMD officer for the Church of England.

Residential training should be challenging because ministry is challenging. During training, ordinands and their families come to recognize more about the personal cost of realized vocation. Ordinands should be committed to a deep and rigorous sense of community for their formation as community is a marker of the Holy Spirit moving in the world. Training for priesthood should be about healing our broken world. While the person in ministry is important, it is the sacramental witness of the church as a whole that is central. There are no boxes to be ticked, just people to be served and loved. The church also has a wider duty of care both to the faithful laity and to those seeking to serve in other ways, such as through education. Theological training colleges do well to heed this and to be open. The diversity at St. Jude's House is challenging and interests me. So, I applied for the post of Vice Principal & Director of Pastoral Studies. So, how do I understand this role at a college known affectionately as Blaggers?

This role in its range of responsibilities is crucial both to the smooth running of the house and to the rigorous development of the ordinands, other inquirers, and students. It is not a role to be lightly undertaken, but is one that would best be done by someone who can combine significant parish ministry with academic integrity. This post also involves the continued opening up of St. Jude's, which is itself a very important institution for the wider vocation of the church through its traditional adherence to the Catholic faith. In these days of economic and social rigor, whatever the backgrounds of the ordinands, most, by their ecclesiology, would be drawn to the inner cities, or areas of urban deprivation. I have much experience to share here. Bringing spiritual beauty through worship and faithful service gives the poor their dignity and restores the *imago Dei* in them.

It is also important to understand the wideness of provision and the range of audiences at St. Jude's, to welcome these factors as they bring the "real world" to the "protected wilderness" of residential formation.

How did I understand my own sense of calling with respect to this post? I started with the questions I would want to ask if I were interviewing for this post. Who am I? What is my relevant experience? How would my personality fit with this post?

I am a pastoral and practical theologian with considerable and varied experience as a parish priest, and I would like to share that richness within the context of St. Jude's House. I have always been active with interests and enterprises beyond the parish base. My sense of vocation embraces all aspects of my person, intellectually, aesthetically, emotionally, and spiritually. Working as Vice Principal & Director of Pastoral Ministry would draw upon and extend my experience. I believe I would be credible in the post.

I am a trained counsellor and social group worker. Incidentally, the Diploma in Applications of Psychology qualifies me as a negotiator, a skill that has fed into my diplomatic strategies and techniques. As well as practical and pastoral theology, I could teach about research methods and the social sciences. My academic experience means I am current, or at least as much as one can ever be in the fast-changing world of education, and would welcome involvement with the PGCE course.

My personal style, as you might expect with my background, is nonconfrontational, nonjudgmental. Within that, I will question a situation rather than a person. I use my counselling skills, but I also relish the cut-and-thrust of debate conducted with respect. I am disciplined, knowing how to pace myself, and can aid others in gaining invaluable work-life balance.

I have demonstrated the ability to change and to promote change. In Lowshire, I was involved with fresh expressions initiatives—church initiatives to establish new or different forms of church for a changing culture. Such practical and professional experiences are useful tools for teaching those in vocational work.

I am told that I am a clear and inspiring preacher. Good preaching needs to use all the modern imagery and symbols as signposts to the deeper meaning of our faith and its continuing relevance. Our starting point is always that internal dialogue with the Holy Spirit, the undergirding of prayer without which ministry is a hollow sham.

What about teaching? Teaching is a process of constantly reinforcing a message and demonstrating how to live it, as the ordinals so clearly indicate. Teaching requires intellectual clarity, but also an ability to differentiate and to use teacher-speak according to who is being taught. Clergy should be able to operate for themselves at the highest level of interrogation of the tradition, but also be able to bring it into the minds of people whose lives need simple, ready reassurance of God's purposes for them. So why was I not interviewed and appointed for this post? I think we know all too well the answer to that question.

Bishops keep files, as one would expect, on all their clergy. These are known as the Blue Files. Clearly, I was not going to be offered a senior or specialist job in the Church of England, but what would happen if I applied for bog standard (ordinary, basic, or mediocre) vicar jobs under the new employment arrangements known as common tenure? The first thing I had to do was find out what sort of reference my bishop was willing to give. Would he be unkind enough to say anything about the failed group ministry that had been blamed on me? I had been in touch with his chaplain seeking some clarification and assurance about this following an interview in Scotland where it had been reflected back to me that conflicting things were being said about my suitability for the post applied for. I emailed the bishop's chaplain requesting access to all the information held in my personal files, as I have a legal right to do. I understood that there might be a fee of not more than £10 payable for this and made it clear that I would be happy to make payment if required. I asked for confirmation of the relevant privacy notice for this diocese relating to the information held. I further sought advice on what course of action to take if I were of the view that any information held on me was factually incorrect.

What about that blue file on me as a member of the clergy that was held in the bishop's office? On a positive note, my file says that I am a faithful, hard-working, catholic priest who is valued by many in a vibrant and multiethnic parish. It was recognized that I am an established and credible academic who has published widely in the field of Black theology. However, on a more negative note, the blue file says that I did not find it easy to work with colleagues in a group ministry, that I flourish best when I am the sole leader. And that is the context in which they believe I can be effective in leadership. There is some truth in this as I don't work well with racist White colleagues who seek to control me.

I saw the advert for North Brightsey. This parish had lost its last incumbent under some very difficult and harrowing circumstances. Child abuse charges had been brought against the vicar and his response had been to take his own life, which received fairly extensive media coverage. I had had experience of taking charge of such a situation in a previous post, so I thought I would apply, thinking I could facilitate a process of healing and restore some integrity to the parish.

There is one gospel but many ways of interpreting it. Above all, I preach that we are all sinners and not one of us can truly stand in judgment of another. That is liberating and helps people come to terms with terrible events such as the deep sadness that this parish had experienced. This bereavement is a complex, genuine loss. In my application I explained that this damaged parish should be enabled to continue to move forward, not being defined by the past, but looking toward the future while being active in the present.

I offered to this post my skills as counsellor with a background in social care, together with a wide and varied parochial ministry. I outlined my experience of entering a new post after a challenging predecessor. I understood how people vary in their emotions to such challenging circumstances, needing one-to-one support. Old-fashioned parish ministry such as strategic, careful visiting can be crucial. Rebuilding is key, and the priest needs pastoral sensitivity as different people obviously have very different needs. Behind all this is my notion that the priest is the meeting place for the vocations of many: a prayerful center ready to empower as well as to console.

A lot of prayerful preparation went into to this application. Given my track record, readers of this book will not be surprised to learn that there was enormous interest in this post and that on this occasion I was not shortlisted for an interview. Nevertheless, they were honored that I applied, or so the public relations talk claimed. The trouble is these posts attract many such high-caliber applications and other candidates were able to demonstrate a greater match to the job specifications and roles. Clearly, I was out of my league, or so they would have me believe. I seem to recall it was the curate from a neighboring parish that was appointed after three years in holy orders.

A similar thing happened at the coastal parish of Chapel End North. Archdeacon Bill Craven, hiding behind his personal assistant, claimed it was clear from my application that I had much to offer the right parish, but that Chapel End North, with its needs and aspirations, was not the right one for me. So, with regret, he had to inform me that I had not been shortlisted for interview. Maybe he was referring to a different parish profile from the one he sent to me. Who can say? The job itself was far from difficult and I guess in due course we will know which junior member of the clergy he wanted to place there. The letter concluded with the archdeacon expressing his warmest thanks for all I had put into exploring this possibility, and his hope was that I would find the right post soon.

So, what about the mystery job? The post nobody would expect me to apply for? Yes, I did apply to be a chaplain at a public school. So, after years of embracing the Magnificat theology of the underdog, would I now dedicate my life to educating the children of the rich and privileged? Seriously, my motivation here was one of challenge. I really wanted to see what their reaction would be to me as a Black priest who had attended a bog-standard comprehensive and now wanted to be their chaplain. So, I applied for the post of School Chaplain at Filbert Vale, whose strapline is—*A great place to learn, follow the narrative.* So, what was the story with these people? Applicants were assured that the procedures used in the recruitment process would not discriminate against suitably qualified persons on the grounds of belief, marital status, sexual orientation, pregnancy, age, sex, disability, race, color, ethnic or national origin, or religion. After covering all bases in this fashion, Filbert Vale then made it very clear that they had the right to appoint a school chaplain at any stage in the recruitment process. So, what was my experience of their recruitment process? What did I learn about the public school system in the UK and its deployment of Black clergy?

I started my application by explaining that the drivers of my vocation are the twin missions of care and development. I wanted them to know that I see the work of a priest as the meeting place of all the vocations of those the priest meets. It is a service that echoes that of St. Martin, from whose famous intervention to the poor man the term "chaplain" is derived. Vocation is both a recognition that we are all needy, but also that we all have God-given strengths that can be nurtured. More to the point, they needed to know that I have been closely involved in schools since my ordination, delivering assemblies to a wide age range and also engaging in small group work, looking at issues related to morality, ethical dilemmas, and preferred behaviors, often using techniques based on values clarification. Again, since ordination, I have been active in the Air Training Corps, and lately also with the Sea Cadets, so I can offer experience and expertise here to those groups supported by the school. One aspect of my work has been enabling other ordained people and lay people to develop a formal ministry through regular contributions to worship. In a school such as Filbert Vale, I would be very keen to continue this as a means of deepening people's faith, whatever their age. I would seek to continue the work of the chapel as a place of quiet and sanctuary in all the busyness of boarding life. With my qualifications and experience in conflict resolution, I would also seek to bring healing and peace into the disquiet that can arise in close communities on an entirely nonjudgmental basis. In my person, as a Black priest, I am a marker of reconciliation and hope in a divided world. So, let our narrative begin.

I started to think about the school profile. Things were missing and I wondered how a competent human resources officer could have allowed such paperwork to leave the office and be put into the public domain. There seemed to be a number of things that would need clarification. I appreciated the college has its own pay scale, but what was it and how would that relate to my situation? If appointed, could I stay within the Church of England pension scheme? Schools are very hierarchical institutions, so where would the chaplain be located in the structure? Would the new chaplain be paid as a head of department? I understood a house would be made available for the new chaplain, but there were no details.

In terms of the life of the chapel, what amount of autonomy would the new chaplain have? What liturgies are already in use? How formal are the services? What kinds of resources already exist? Who else is in involved, including students? Does the chaplain prepare students for confirmation if need be? In curricular terms, what schemes of work already exist? Some samples might have been helpful. Would the new chaplain be expected to teach all faiths, and what artifacts—by this I mean teaching aids and curriculum resources such as teaching packs—support this? Might there be the possibility to bring speakers in, especially those of other world faiths? How feasible, given location, would visits to significant religious sites be? How are budgets delegated both to the chapel and to the subject heads?

As it turned out I never got an answer to any of these questions. What I did get was an email from the HR officer, Lyre Harper, informing me that they were not taking my application any further. I was also told that the decision had been a difficult one, as the overall standard of candidates was high. A week later they re-advertised the post. I don't think there were any other candidates. I can only conclude that they were not ready for a Black school chaplain. Filbert Vale—*A great place to learn, follow the narrative.*

What about parishes where I was interviewed? Was the feedback any different? An application to South Bareham on the north coast resulted in an interview at the bishop's palace. My wife, Linda, and I then had to travel some considerable distance to visit the parish. The person who showed us around the vicarage wouldn't even look at me and addressed their comments to Linda. The feedback from Archdeacon Jill Buckingham was that they had serious concerns that, in my then post, I was the safeguarding officer and not one of the active lay members. Was this the only reason for not appointing me? It is perfectly reasonable for the vicar of an inner-city parish to fulfill this role by default. I thought this type of feedback was rich coming from a diocese that was under investigation for the alleged cover-up of child abuse.

At East Ascot, I spent a pleasant afternoon with churchwardens and active lay people engaging in much conversation and fellowship. However, following a formal interview with presentations I was told by the archdeacon, Rocky Pine, that the fit was just not right between me and this parish. It was a matter of chemistry. It was a good application, you understand. I was an applicant with a clear sense of vocation and many gifts both spiritual and theological. I was told that I had a good sense of humor, with a calm and gentle personality. Furthermore, I had good verbal communication skills, but I was not the right person for this post because they needed someone who could drive the needs of the parish forward. They wanted someone who could offer on-the-ground expertise and leadership skills. They wanted a direct and down-to-earth White man with not too many qualifications to tell them what to do. Clearly, they did not want a pastorally orientated Black priest who had no blueprint but wanted to work with them and the Holy Spirit to move God's kingdom forward. Well, I got it wrong again.

At the parish of Newville, there was an interesting social divide between the middle-class archdeacon and bishop and the two White, working-class churchwardens who were clearly uncomfortable with me and incapable of articulating coherent and relevant questions as to my ability to do the job. Did they understand the vicar's role in the context of Newville? Living in this town had been described in a local video as worse than getting herpes. The interview took place at the bishop's house, far removed from the deprivation of Newville. To cut a long story very short, I didn't get the job. The archdeacon, Ruby Carr, thanked me for applying and let me down gently by commenting on my academic achievements. It sounded a bit like what I read in my blue file.

I wrote to the bishop thanking him for the many positive comments and endorsements I found in my blue file. I went on to say I did however have one concern based upon his analysis of my ability to work collaboratively. I wanted the bishop to understand that such work has been a major driver of my ministry as evinced by a long track record. The issues I faced upon my arrival in Brougham seven years earlier were very specific to time and persons. Time moved on and the various persons dispersed. I continued to work in a variety of teams in a range of contexts. I provided the bishop with an addendum that I respectfully requested be added to his reference if he was not able to remove or amend his comments.

When I was appointed to the post of vicar of St. Philip's in 2009, it was widely noted that I was the first Black incumbent in this diverse inner-city parish, even earning a mention in the national press. I perceived the White clergy group as hostile from the interview onwards. I should add that I was not the only clergy colleague to find them difficult. One of the ministers in secular employment was reduced to tears by them so much so that this colleague's spouse referred to them as "the cabal." This colleague then left. Their group mindset made any meaningful interaction problematic. This is not an unheard-of phenomenon by any means, and much energy and research has been put into this by communication theory experts.

The group collectively and individually treated me as though I was their junior, as if I had been a curate rather than a parish priest for many years. The tone of the dialogue between us became increasingly tense. When group events were due to happen under St. Philip's aegis, I was always told what to do and who would be doing what in the service or event. When I asked about other group events happening elsewhere, I was informed it was down to the incumbent of the particular church, and that it essentially had nothing to do with me. This lack of reciprocity was noted by my congregation, many of whom were highly perceptive after living for years in a White-majority country.

It is also worth noting that whilst members of the other churches attended our annual big event of the Caribbean evening, no White stipendiary clergy from the group ever saw fit to enjoy our fellowship.

It was further noted by my parishioners that an important training event put on by the highly qualified Diocesan Racial Justice Officer, that was organized to help White clergy interact with Black people, was avoided by the rest of the clergy in the group. This was regarded as a telling statement, and the officer concerned recorded this in one of her publications.

These examples may seem small, but the spiritual and emotional impact of such encounters made for a very draining time. I felt increasingly torn by my wish to be professionally loyal to my clergy colleagues and the necessity to acknowledge my congregation's concerns.

I hope this gives you something of the journey that I went on. I trust that you can see that, however others viewed me, I viewed them optimistically until I could do so no longer and was forced, by circumstances, to make a stand.

CHAPTER THREE

BLACK CLERGY, WHITE CLERGY, AND PURPLE BISHOPS

THE PURPOSE OF THIS chapter is to relate my own experiences of the Church of England with those of other clergy. I do this through a review and significant update of research I carried out during the 1990s as part of my PhD dissertation concerning the mode of involvement of Black Christians in the Church of England.[1] I was concerned with identifying the dominant themes that emerged, and to offer some interpretations of the ways that different groups of clergy and bishops experience and construct the world of the Church of England. My focus was the extent to which perceptions could be related to an agenda about English ethnicity being the driving force for the deployment of Black clergy in the Church of England.

Some research participants felt that Black worshippers identified with Anglican liturgy because of the Church of England's colonial past:

> As an Anglican, I identify with it because that is what I was baptized into. And so, it is my spiritual home. Coming out of the Caribbean, I have also experienced

1. Isiorho, "Black Clergy Discontent," 213–26.

Pentecostal worship. But the tradition within the Anglican church is what I was brought up in. And so that feels like home and that's what I identify with. It is what I had in the Caribbean and it's what is here which is the same. (RP25)

And:

The older generation will still feel at home because the church and its culture here was transported over to the West Indies. I clearly remember as a child, just before I was 10, where there was this church where we used to meet in this lady's house. It was a big house with massive lawns, and once a month they used to have a church service there. Now my grandmother used to take me to another church where a White priest used to come once a month from the capital. Yes, Afro Caribbean people would identify with the *Book of Common Prayer* and Hymns Ancient and Modern. (RP28)

This Caribbean tradition of Anglican worship is an important but difficult notion to explore because research participants do not really explain what they mean. Clearly, it involves the *Book of Common Prayer*, but what are the connotations, and what do they, as Anglicans, think of Pentecostalism? Amongst the Black laity, there was open hostility to independent Black churches. In marked contrast, the majority of the Black clergy did not see themselves in competition with Pentecostal churches. Some of the Black clergy shared their church buildings with Pentecostalists and saw this as a normal ecumenical venture involving the occasional joint service. Other clergy had to struggle with this, and here relationships were not so cordial. However, the overall feeling was that competition was not necessary because what the Church of England was offering people in the cities and urban areas of deprivation was so different from that of independent Black churches.

Some research participants thought that the liturgy ought to be changed and made more accessible. They linked liturgical change with a widening of the definition of Englishness.

Thus:

> I think without a doubt the Anglican church is in one
> sense very English because it is the package of the Gospel
> through English or British eyes. So, I think it is unavoid-
> able for them to be anything else, but an expression of
> Englishness. I think however for Black people to survive
> within that, it is not just to see the church as an expres-
> sion of Englishness but perhaps to see the link with other
> parts of the Anglican Communion and to separate the
> package from the message. If we can do this, we can make
> the Church of England ours also and change the face of
> it, so that it is no longer an Englishness that is described
> as White but becomes multi-cultural and multi ethnic. In
> other words, changing the face of Anglicanism. The fact
> is that Anglicanism has been taken out to other parts of
> the world. We can show a brand of Anglicanism which
> has integrity, but Anglicanism through our eyes, though
> our experiences. We are still valuing the tradition and
> the message, but we are endowing it with our culture and
> our way of life and our way of thinking. (RP25)

Many of my research participants felt that older Black people
might come back to the Church of England if there was the right
sort of encouragement for them to do so. However, it was felt that
the younger generation experienced a similar alienation from the
ethos of the church, which has been the experience of many White
young people in English society. The generational factors here are
very important. The older people may well come back to a church
that is relevant to the worshippers who came to Britain from the
Caribbean. However, to make this work, the church would need
to recruit a lot more Black clergy, not only as parish priests, but
also as archdeacons and bishops. When predominantly Black areas
of the UK require a new bishop, experienced Black clergy should
dominate the short list. But it does not work like that because of
the deep and unacknowledged racism of the Church of England. It
is so clear that to get ordained as a Black Christian you have to be
head and shoulders above your White counterparts. So, don't tell

me that there are not sufficient, able Black clergy to take up these posts, because that would be a wicked lie.

My starting point was Black clergy discontent with the structures of the Church of England. And here there seems to be a distinct sense of generation within the Black clergy sampled. Some process of separation has occurred since the arrival in the UK of the immigrants of the fifties and sixties who thought that they belonged. Some long process of disillusionment is at work. The older clergy, those who were in the last stages of their ministry, said how undervalued they were and how unused they felt by the church. There is a lot of pain and hostility in what they have to say. Clearly, they have things to offer and the church does not want to know about them. This is a very serious indictment of the work of the church in the cities and urban areas of deprivation, where most Black clergy are to be found.

The sentiment is that the longer you are here, the more you feel outside, and the younger generation are part of a secular society for whom church participation is irrelevant. Thus, the church does not feature as a significant factor in this sense of exclusion in the UK. Young people, in terms of youth culture, and particularly young Black people, are more into the mainstream because of the music industry and the media, which is a particularly sinister form of exploitation. Black chic is still fashionable, the black shades and baseball cap, etc. The older generation do not have to contend with that in the same kind of way.

The majority of White research participants, like their Black colleagues, expressed the view that the Church of England was maintaining a Christian presence in the cities and in urban areas of deprivation. However, this group did not profess the same enthusiasm for *Faith in the City* although they were more willing to use the term "inner-city." This Christian presence was often identified as Anglican and English. Research participants recognized that Black worshippers had in the past been excluded from these structures. There was also some recognition of institutionalized racism in the contemporary affairs of church and state. Emphasis was placed upon the importance of maintaining resources in deprived areas and, for some research participants, this was a way of demonstrating the church's relevance in a modern world. The church's activities are described in the language of outreach and mission. Thus, the cities and urban areas of deprivation were not to be abandoned lest the Church of England should lose its credibility there and everywhere else.

Research participants also talked about the changing class structure of the Church of England in relation to its sense of Englishness. The inner-city role was related to power struggles within the church between those who wanted innovation in the mode of decision making and in liturgy and the old-style leadership which resided at the center. There was considerable dissatisfaction with this group who were identified as reactionary elements within the church. This group included church civil servants. There was less criticism of the bishops from the White clergy than there had been from their Black counterparts.

These research participants had no difficulty providing a considerable list of things they understood the church was doing in the cities and urban areas of deprivation. These included supported church schools, attracting grants from other organizations as well as deploying its own resources, maintaining its buildings, maintaining clergy in those areas, looking for new forms and styles of worship, and keeping the mission work of the church alive for the local communities they were supporting.

Thus:

> I think the Church of England is in a better position than anyone else in the sense that it possesses buildings and it's expected to be present and is looked for to be present, and frequently is. And it is in a position to deploy a certain amount of financial resources of its own and to attract grants from other bodies. I think because we are quite a large church it is possible to have clergy in these places even if there is a rapid turn-over because of stress. At least it is a presence. I think we ought not to forget the Church of England schools which again make a not insignificant inner-city contribution. Some of these schools can have an 80 percent or 90 percent content,

which is quite amazing and does create some obvious difficulties for everyone concerned, but it seems to be the case that people still value the existence of such places. (RP33)

As far as I can see, looking from the outside in, it is trying to support local communities, to keep the church and the mission of the church alive in those areas. And I think the biggest problem that it has is adapting itself to a new way of working. That its structure, its traditional structure, is not in my view flexible enough in many ways to meet the challenge. So, in some places where the church is willing to change and adapt readily it works quite well. In other places, where it is a bit more traditional it doesn't work well. One of the failings of the church in the past it seems to me is that we tend to ask people to meet us where we are, so we ask them to come and be like us, which for the Church of England traditionally has been White middle class. That attitude and mode of thinking has got to change because people will no longer meet us where we are, we've got to meet them wherever they are. And that is the gap that the Church of England is trying, with different methods, to bridge in the inner-cities. (RP32)

There was a considerable similarity between what research participants believed the Church of England was doing and what they felt it should be doing in the cities and urban areas of deprivation. Research participants wanted more mission and outreach which would include help for the poor and the underprivileged. Some research participants did feel that the Church of England should be asking political questions about the distribution of resources and acting as a bridge between the poor and those in positions of authority. Only one research participant expressed the view that the Church of England was wasting its resources in the cities and urban areas of deprivation. The thrust of this argument is that the church is engaging in self-congratulatory campaigns which direct community energies into nonthreatening and apolitical projects. Thus, *Faith in the City* can only result in the alienation of people from the institution of the church.

There is this sense of "We are doing good, and we must congratulate ourselves," and the workers are all busy working with each other but not working with the people. When you want certain practical things, they want to come across with the goods. If you want to set up a motorcycle circuit for young offenders, you find they would prefer to set up something like free access to libraries. I don't actually know of any good project involving the Church of England in the inner-cities. (RP31)

There were considerably more references to the church's mission or outreach than there was to *Faith in the City*. Research participants were selective about which aspects of this program they wanted to see developed and they made their choices with little consideration of the difficulties that would and should face the church as a change agent. Their theology did not really go beyond "Let us be kind to the urban poor." However, the language of inner-city projects was evident and provided justification for the church's continual presence. Research participants understood the church's role to champion the poor by providing resource centers and engaging in a certain amount of community work in order to gain credibility. This in turn would make the church accessible to the helpless and, with the introduction of user-friendly liturgy, bring people into church. There was also a strong feeling that this Christian presence had to be defended rather than defined:

It has a presence simply because there are parish priests in most places still. However, the squeeze is on financially to maintain this presence in the poorer areas. (RP34)

The first thing that it's doing is being there. And that I think is the most fundamental. And whatever one says about it, that fact that they are there and that we are hopefully the one thing we are committed to is not to withdraw from those areas however poor the response might be. And I find being part of a congregation of 40 of whom half are over 70 in a parish of 15,000 indicates that we are committed to being there. And our influence is disproportionate to our size because of that. There are a lot of specific projects in the urban areas done by many churches. Those I am sure have a considerable value. In terms of being there, the Church of England is probably the best of the lot. Because of our liturgy and our fairly fixed forms of worship, it is difficult for those of non C of E backgrounds to be brought in and an increasing number are of non C of E background. I think of the Family Service we have tried to get going in our inner-city parish. For a short time, it took off, for about a year, and it's now almost run into the ground. And very few people, additional people, are coming to the Family Service. I think this has to do with difficulties over worship. The fact is that the older people are extremely resistant to change to the pattern of worship. And can be positively unwelcoming to the younger people if they think the younger people want to change things. And I find this very disturbing. I think we are more and more as clergy, and an increasing number of lay people, are beginning to come to see as true that wide ranging changes have got to take place. (RP30)

The language of the deprived city included the term "inner-city," but not "urban priority area," and this has implications for two of our hypotheses, namely, that "The Church of England's use of the phrase Urban Priority Area (UPA) is a coded term for talking about Black people and 'race-related issues,'" and that "The higher the social group within the Anglican hierarchy, the more the inner-city concept will be perceived as Black." Consider the comments of the following research participants:

The most obvious thing that the Church of England is doing because of its very parochial nature, is that it is enabling a Christian presence to be in the urban areas and the inner-cities . . . And I would be a strong advocate of wanting the Church of England to continue to provide resources for the inner-city areas. (RP29)

I think an important thing that we are doing in the inner-city is learning . . . I think we are taking on board our duties in the inner-city, but it is a slow process. (RP30)

> We ought to be forming the bridge between the folk in
> the inner-cities who feel that they have been forgotten
> and rejected and pushed to the edges of society, we ought
> to be a bridge between them and the rest of society.
> (RP32)

> And since it is virtually inconceivable that we should pull
> out of the suburbs, which after all cough up the quota
> which enable the whole machine to survive, it is going to
> be the case that we pull out of the countryside or pull out
> of the inner-city to an increasing extent. (RP33)

However, one research participant equated "inner-city" to
White communities in the East End of London which is interesting because there is also a large Bengali population which was not
mentioned:

> We should be finding out who we are and then keeping
> in contact with the leaders of many disparaged commu-
> nities that our inner-cities are made up of because there
> has been one big sociological change. A hundred years
> ago the inner-city was far more poverty stricken and
> hungry than it is now. But it was a unity, the East Ender
> knew where he came from. Today, even in one inner-city
> parish, we have lots of little groups who don't know what
> is happening fifty doors away from them. (RP30)

Research participants raised the issue of racial injustice
which they related to the mechanisms of exclusion within the
church as well as society at large. Research participants preferred
to blame the system rather than the quality of leadership provided
by senior officeholders. White research participants, unlike their
Black counterparts, did not stress the importance of Black leadership within the church. Only one research participant criticized
the bishops, whilst one other advocated the need for more Black
bishops.

Research participants talked about the exclusion of Black
worshippers and all of them were highly committed to challenging
such injustice as part of their work in the cities and urban areas of
deprivation. This led some research participants to criticize church

structures that perpetuate racialized injustices. The following two extracts concern church schools:

> In 1984, a school in a White highland area was threatened with closure, they instructed a lawyer and fought the case and won. When the local politics changed, a successful school in a poorer area was closed. The rich school now has children from the poor area going to it. The school has not got a good reputation, there are staffing difficulties, and it didn't pass its Ofsted. The neighboring church-aided school was asked to be alongside them and help it to raise its standards. The plan now is to make this school into another church-aided school. This is all very well, but we have to look at admission criteria, which, as a church school, could be defined by geographical area. The catchment area will include two parishes on the one hand and a deanery on the other. Three quarters of one of the parishes is White highlands and the other brings in the children from the successful one which was closed. You can weight the criteria one way or another. You can weight it so that it becomes a successful school, or you can weight it so that the poor can succeed in it. The church is not grasping nettles in terms of mission and prophetic voice saying "No, we won't do that because it is unjust." What is happening is that the church is going for success in the world's terms. It is more about the poor than race, but it is very difficult to get children of other faiths into church schools. The question in my mind is this: Is the church actually replicating the values of the world? (RP34)

> School A is taking over School B. Now some of us in the inner-city are very happy that there shall be a second Church of England school—a secondary school. The other faith communities are not unhappy that there should be a second Church of England secondary school. But the other faith communities are saying, and we are saying from my parish, that if we are true to the vision of *Faith in the City* that this secondary school should be aimed primarily at the residents of the inner-city whereas we suspect it is being aimed, not entirely but primarily,

at the residents of the leafy suburbs. That is an example where we feel that the diocesan structures are not actually seeing the inner-city as the key thing, but rather they are content to carry on in the old way. (RP30)

White research participants were reluctant to use the word "racism" even though they recognized some of its mechanisms. We can only speculate as to why they should hold back from naming it. We can argue that this group of research participants were conscious of their own culpability as White people in English society in the operation of a policy of exclusion. The natural inclination is not to declare your own culpability, and so the word "racism" is not used. Clearly, people do not always differentiate between collective responsibility and individual guilt especially where defense mechanisms are in operation.

Discussions about class were often related to a notion of Englishness:

> And it seems to me that the Church of England is fighting a rear-guard action to defend its Englishness on several fronts. This is one of the reasons why what I call a Radio Two culture of people who were into the Alternative Service Book and in to "Oh yes, Jesus, you are a real guy—let's give you a round of applause." This is not middle-class England that is speaking, it is not those who promoted Empire, who maintain Monarchy, who like to think they can deal with polysyllables. It's actually the voice of the masses much more than the Church of England can bear to accept. (RP31)

I think Englishness is a myth because our society is not monochrome. Englishness is things which the White middle class consider to be a perfect society. Some people spend a lot of time trying to find this. We see this when people who have been brought up in the suburbs or in the cities move up in social class and then move out into the country where they try to make a country village into a typical concept of what England is supposed to be about. They try and make the society there an English society. They will never actually achieve it because they are grasping at something which doesn't exist. Sometimes you sadly find parish churches that seem to be more interested in Englishness than they are in God, where the people are much more Churchians than they are Christians. But these are in the minority and the economic pressure in society, if nothing else, is diminishing their numbers all the time. I think it has been a long time since the Church of England was the Tory party at prayer, a very long time; probably not since the Second World War has that been true. But there is still the unfortunate tendency which I mentioned earlier of trying to assimilate people to a certain culture, a middle-class culture, within the church, but again that is breaking down. We are much better at accepting people as they are than we used to be, although there are still cliques within churches. There are few churches now that anyone would walk into and think that this is the center of Englishness on earth. I think the Church of England has two faces: the real face across the country, which is very varied and changing and moving on, and secondly there is the stereotypical face, which is in the minds of the popular press and people who don't go to church. There is a credibility gap between the two. We have only to look at the way the clergy were portrayed until recently in the popular press and TV. There is a tremendous gap between what we know to be the truth about clergy and what they in the press thought it was.

The senior hierarchy of the church have a different understanding than the parishes concerning the role of clergy. And this is partly to do with the inflexibility of structures. Some cathedrals see their role as the preservers of this Englishness, or whatever you would like to call it. And they do this against the overwhelming tide of change. Even though the parochial base of the church has changed dramatically, there are, within the church, conservative elements. Take, for example, Church House in London. It would seem to me that the majority of people who work there are retired civil servants whose expressed purpose is to make sure that the church does not veer too far away from the establishment point of view. That's what they are about. Introducing new ideas or trying to change their ideas of Englishness and what it means is very difficult indeed:

At General Synod, by and large, you can introduce new
ideas there. That is the only way of changing church civil
servants is by putting pressure on them through General
Synod. If you can get enough Synod members to make a
fuss, then you can make these people think again. Otherwise they see their role as preservation of the status
quo and making sure that the gap between Parliament
and the church does not widen. And that's something
to do with Englishness as well, I think. Which is all tied
up with this very old notion of establishment, which is a
peculiar thing. I don't know whether it is peculiar to the
English way of doing things. I think we are coming to the
crunch about that with the activities of our Royal Family
at the moment, or some members of it any way. We have
to rethink what establishment means altogether and
that's going to take another pillar away from this myth of
Englishness. (RP32)

These extracts have implications for our first two hypotheses,
namely that The Church of England is a signifier of Englishness
as much as it is of theism, and that the relationship between the
Church of England and the Afro-Caribbean community is determined by a political agenda which has its origin in English ethnicity. Both of these hypotheses were upheld. There was a concern
with maintaining church structure and the characteristics of that
structure was a point of contention between competing groups.
The political agenda was not theistic but cultural, involving issues
of ethnicity and class. One research participant identified a class
of people in the church who were reactionary and opposed to any
form of change. These church civil servants operated from the
center and were in conflict with the General Synod, the church's
parliament. They were identified as a certain class of people occupying a definite position within the English class system. They also
had a definite history. They were the retired generals who had always been around in the church and knew how to move in church
circles. Another group of people are identified as innovative and
aspiring, and some of them are young. There is also something in
here about the tension between rural and urban areas: the people

who move out of towns and pretend that the countryside is the only place to live.

The majority of the White Anglican bishops who were interviewed expressed the view that the Church of England had an important role to play in the cities and urban areas of deprivation, and that this was linked to the position of the church within English society at this time. Like the clergy, they felt that the church was maintaining a presence through its parish structures and by its support for urban projects. Thus, the church had responded to the more recent challenge of urban life through the work of the Church Urban Fund.

Some of the themes raised by the bishops were identical with those of other sample groups. These included: the perceived need for greater Black involvement on church committees, both as lay people and as ordained clergy; the need for more multicultural worship; generational differences in the mode of involvement with independent Black churches attracting younger worshippers; a recognition that independent Black churches had come about as a result of racial discrimination in the Church of England; that racial exclusion was related to structured inequality and class factors; and the club mentality of the established church.

The bishops also raised issues that were not a feature of other sample groups. They spoke more openly about racism as a structured inequality within the Church of England and about their own theological position as a response to that. However, a lot of this reflection took place within the context of the idea that learning about other cultures and treating them with empathy was sufficient as an effective challenge to racial disadvantage. Some of the bishops wanted to break out of this paradigm by looking at global issues that would be relevant to the needs of the universal church and not just the Church of England. The concept of racial justice was introduced toward the end of the interview process.

The bishops introduced the idea of training as a practical way of increasing the level of Black participation. They also recognized the strong Black presence in some city churches and advocated the use of more conferences and gatherings to affirm the gifts of Black worshippers. They also talked about employment practices within church structures as well as within society. One of the dominant themes was racial awareness training for White clergy. This was located clearly within a multicultural framework and there was some confusion between personal relations and power relations.

Research participants were asked to comment on how the Church of England had responded to the challenge of the *Faith in the City* report. Only one of the five bishops interviewed mentioned the follow-up reports to *Faith in the City*, and only two of the bishops used the terminology of Urban Priority Areas:

> I do think there has been some very good things as a result of *Faith in the City*. We have certainly got the cities and the UPAs on the agenda. And in many ways, they have remained on the agenda . . . I think if you actually look at the two follow-on reports it is quite clear that some of the aims and recommendations of "Faith in the City" have actually been carried through. (RP38)

> We have signaled our commitment to maintaining the church in the city and have created two new training posts for deacons. So, we have curates who are going to be trained in what are inner-city areas or urban Priority Areas. (RP39)

Clearly the urban experience was closely related to the Black presence in British society, and this has implications for our hypothesis that the higher the social group within the Anglican hierarchy, the more the inner-city concept will be perceived as Black. Among research participants, there was a perceived association between urban areas, deprivation, and Black British communities, with bishops occasionally using the term "urban priority area," and clergy preferring the term "inner-city." However, there was insufficient evidence to suggest that such a connection was greater among bishops than it had been for clergy or laity. Connections were also made with racial justice issues. It was also felt that the Church Urban Fund had allowed the church to maintain its presence and commitment to these areas and had been responsible for keeping the issues of urban deprivation on the agenda. This had also made it possible to maintain clergy morale in difficult working environments.

Support for the Church Urban Fund was not complete. Bishops did not always agree with the decisions of this organization, but nevertheless valued its work:

> Now I don't always agree with the decisions which it makes. But it is there as a significant ongoing resource within the urban world. The other thing which the Church of England has managed to maintain is a ministry to the whole of England including the inner-city areas, although we are often very stretched. In comparison with other denominations, the Church of England has stayed there when others have pulled out. So, I would say we have stayed stuck into the inner-city. (RP37)

One bishop felt that the response of the church to the urban poor should be that of a long-term commitment which could not be provided by a series of short-term projects:

> I am actually quite critical of the direction which CUF is taking in that in many ways I think it is rather than being empowering, the danger is that it is actually beginning to contribute to a dependency culture. I also have criticisms with its concern for short-term funding. Most of CUF's funding is short term. Now for me, the Gospel is about long-term commitment. This was the great thrust of *Staying in the City*. It is about ongoing presence. This is a theological issue. It is about how God relates to us. He gave himself to us long term. This is actually also an extremely practical issue. My experience of urban ministry has been that true empowering actually takes time, it takes a very long time. (RP38)

All the bishops interviewed talked about the church's commitment to the cities and urban areas of deprivation. The idea that the church might pull out of the cities was not a realistic consideration for this sample group. However, research participants preferred to talk about their particular diocese rather than to comment upon the position of the Church of England as a whole:

We have developed a number of projects in this diocese, the most exciting of which is in a parish where the
church building was knocked down before it fell down.
We have got Millennium funding and the diocese has put
in a quarter of a million of its own on the share extra,
and work is about to start at the end of the year to build
a brand-new worship center, community center, vicarage, and hopefully, in the long term, the rather old local
authority first school on the same or adjacent site will
also be renewed. This is an area of considerable poverty,
unemployment and also a high Asian element. And this
project has explicit support from Muslims and people of
all races and backgrounds in that area. The council have
also put a lot of money in. This is one of the flag ships,
one of the biggest things that we have done. We are in
the process of encouraging a lot of other projects and
have gained Church Urban Fund support for them, quite
a number, and some of them are in conjunction with
the Methodists and we are looking for ways of working
together. So, we continue to take "Faith in the City" very
seriously indeed. And we have deliberately tried to maintain the same number of clergy in inner-city parishes
irrespective of the percentage of Asian population. And
at a time when we are having to cut the number of paid
clergy quite dramatically. (RP39)

Research participants were asked a number of questions
about their role as bishops in promoting policies that were likely to
address the racialized inequalities and disadvantages which were a
feature of church structures. Bishops were asked what they thought
could be done to encourage Black involvement in the Church of
England. The majority of research participants recognized the lack
of involvement which this question implied. They felt that it was
down to them to appoint Black people with abilities to important
posts and that this would have to be backed up with an extensive
program of education to combat racism. Thus they could do this
through a conscious nurturing of Black leadership, and at the same
time speaking out against racism in society.

Research participants were asked why they thought that the Church of England had been unable to attract more young Black people into its ordained ministry. Clearly the church had problems attracting young people, per se. Bishops felt that too much emphasis in the past had been placed upon experience but that what was needed now was more young ordinations. Two of the bishops in this sample group also felt that there may well be some bias in the church's selection procedures which could disadvantage Black applicants, and that there was a club mentality within the church which could be related to Englishness to which Black people did not have access:

> The same kind of glass ceiling that applies in other institutions can be found in the church for similar reasons. They are to do with familiarity: Are you a member of the club? Do you know the rules? Those subtle and nonsubtle ways in which racial discrimination expresses itself. (RP35)

It was recognized by the majority of our sample group that there was a considerable lack of appropriate role models to encourage Black people to put themselves forward for ordination. Having come forward, it would then be necessary for changes to be made to theological training to take in account the importance of Black history. It was generally felt that the situation had been greatly improved as a result of the ministry of the church's three Black bishops. However, the bishops felt that there was no room for complacency and that selection and appointment procedures would have to be made more open. It was noted that there was a considerable lack of Black representation in middle management concerning the appointment of Black archdeacons and cathedral deans. Here again, the bishops felt that this could only be addressed by giving Black clergy the opportunities to experience the type of ministry that was likely to lead to a senior appointment. Two of the bishops felt that the position of Black Britons was more disadvantaged than that of those who came here from other churches within the Anglican communion.

One comments thusly:

Often the people with the greatest clarity in these matters have I think been Anglo Indians of one kind or another. Afro Caribbean have much more difficulty in getting accepted . . . I worked closely when I was in London with a particular priest. He is somebody who is an articulate, gifted, Indian person who I suspect the race issues came upon the day later in his consciousness whereas if he had been Afro Caribbean it would have been on his pulse from the start. He has since experienced racism in this country. (RP35)

And another:

I think that Black British find it more difficult than Black Asian people who have come here more recently from abroad. I think that Black people from abroad have a greater confidence and a greater freedom of their own sense of can-do ability. And Black British people have been through the discrimination process from the time that they were quite young. And I think they have internalized a greater sense of a lack of confidence. And it is more difficult for them. And they tend to be more retiring. That is a difficult problem. When we had the last General Synod, we did offer training for people, we put on a training day for candidates to encourage Black and Asian candidates. This was useful, it was good for all candidates. We didn't just do it for Black candidates. (RP36)

The bishops were asked if they felt it would be a useful strategy to increase the representation of Black people on the Bishop's Council, a policymaking body of the church. The majority of bishops thought this would be a good idea and that it was most likely to happen through co-options rather than elections.

However, one of the bishops thought that this would lead to tokenism and commented thusly:

As far as Bishop's Council is concerned or the diocesan synod, it is really up to the people to get themselves organised and push themselves forward or push people forward from their own communities. That's about democracy. You get on Bishop's Council by an election. Yes,

I am sure it would be a good thing to increase the Black representation on the Bishop's Council as long as it is not just tokenism and that the Bishop's Council gives itself time to hear what is said by any representatives of the Black community who are there. (RP.37)

Another bishop, meanwhile, echoing the tokenism theme, thought the whole strategy would work better in dioceses other than his own on account of its size:

In a diocese that has very few Black Christians, the danger is tokenism. We have got to look respectable, so we need a Black face. What we need to do is to find out what people's skills are and try to use those skills and experience appropriately, which is what I have done with my selectors for example. The person that I have asked to become a selector is a person of considerable experience. She happens to be Black. We have to be a bit careful that we don't fall into tokenism. What I can do is to encourage a parish to choose and encourage people for appropriate jobs. We need to find out about their skills and then to see how they can be encouraged and supported in doing that. If you do put somebody in because they are Black it may show your concern, but I don't actually think it is very helpful. If you can put somebody in because they got those gifts and they happen to be Black, then you won twice I think. So, in a diocese like this, we need a relatively patient educative system of making people aware that these people are as much British and part of the Church of England as you or I and may well have lived here longer. It is a question here of patience. In a larger diocese where there are larger numbers, then there, I think, the Bishop's Council is a body with a very real responsibility because there the structures are much more important. If you have got thousands of people, then structures matter. Providing it is done with the good will of Black Anglicans then I think building in some kind of presence in the structures is very important . . . Again, I would say that if you have people of ability, yes. I would be reluctant to do it by building in a quota of Black representation. I would want to try and educate

the Bishop's Council and the diocesan synod from which
the Bishop's Council are elected, to see how important a
step that would be, and voluntarily go out and try and
encourage people to stand and offer to give their support.
As a bishop I am not allowed to interfere with the election of the clergy or the laity, but I can say to somebody,
"Look, he or she is a very good person and I wonder if
you could encourage them to stand for election." (RP39)

Yet another bishop felt that it would be good if more than one
person was co-opted on to the Bishop's Council as they would have
the opportunity of working together to bring about some kind of
change. This bishop commented thusly:

Yes, as long as there is more than one. I think we need
several people who can make common cause if they want
to. I think that would be very good. It would change the
dynamic of the Bishop's Council. I am not sure how you
would do it because members have to be elected. And
candidates have to be willing to stand. Maybe we need
a bit more positive encouragement in that area just as in
the General Synod elections. (RP36)

Research participants felt that the Church of England should
do more than just foster good race relations with independent
Black churches and other faith communities. The response of the
church to these communities had to also include racial justice issues like the cause of asylum seekers and discrimination in the
workplace. Research participants tended to relate the concept of
racial justice not to the church as an institution, but rather as a
challenge to the church in combating racism in society at large:

People coming from different parts of Africa and seeking asylum here are in touch with church groups and
the Center for Black and White Christian Fellowship.
So, there are those kinds of involvement. I think that all
that's important. But to go back to SRB (single regeneration budget). One reason why this is so important is because if the employment situation for young Black people
which I believe is considerable worse than for their White
counterparts. So additional training resources which are

focused upon minority ethnic groups seem to be entirely right. (RP37)

Research participants also talked about racial justice as a theological concept:

> Issues of empowerment and of celebration and articulation, I think we are still having to fight to ensure they remain on the agenda. Empowerment isn't just to do with empowerment in the local situation, it is actually to do with empowerment within the whole people of God and is therefore to do with the liberation of the people of God. The church becomes what it is called to be, and all the people of God are able to make their full contribution. CUF will never achieve its full potential until CUF trustees are themselves representative of the range of church membership, including people from UPAs. This organization needs to have members on its board from UPAs to be effective. That UPA experience has much to offer to the whole work of CUF and it then actually begins to affect the whole way in which CUF can make its contrition, not just to UPAs, but to the wider church. We must not lose the focus of the priority area, but actually if we are going to take seriously the priority area, we need to look at the whole area of urbanization and city life. (RP38)

> Justice is one mark of the kingdom of God. What I increasingly hope to do is to sensitize people in parishes, particularly those who can be said to live in the White highlands, to realize that it is their responsibility as much as anybody else. Justice is something that applies to them. (RP39)

The theological dimension allowed research participants to integrate their concern about racism in society with their responsibility as key officeholders for an institution within that society. The more theological this discussion became, the less it was bound up with maintaining an involvement with the institutions of good race relations. Employment issues in society could be related to employment issues in the church. Opposing government policy of immigration law was not an alternative to tackling the isolation of church congregations from the wider church community. The appointment of specialist officers, fostering new Black ministries, presenting the church as an international community, listening to and empowering the powerless, and looking critically at issues of national identity, these were all part of the church's prophetic role.

Black clergy from across one diocesan area in this sample group believed that the established church was a presence for Christian witness in the cities and urban areas of the UK, proclaiming the gospel through outreach programs such as that provided by the Church Urban Fund. Guided by the *Faith in the City* report, there was an optimism about the church's relevance to the inner city. In this context, church services and buildings would become more accessible to the community the church was trying to serve. However, it soon became evident that not all Black clergy thought that community-based projects were wide enough or sufficiently funded to sustain that Christian presence. Some Black colleagues felt that the church was drifting into a false understanding of itself as just another agency working alongside many others for the common good and that its liturgical focus had somehow been diminished. For this group of Black clergy, there was a real choice between the church as a serving community of faith on the one hand, and the church as the worshipping community of faith on the other. However, the majority of Black clergy gave focus to the traditional role of the priest within the Anglican community and did not see this as a contradiction in any way to working with people through state institutions and voluntary agencies.

Most clergy in the cities and urban areas had open policies regarding baptisms, weddings, and funerals, and they saw these services as important points of contact between the community and the church. Research participants felt clergy should be more approachable and ready to listen to the poor. This would help clergy to become more effectively the voice of the voiceless. Thus clergy would have a genuine role alongside the poor, offering a real challenge to the wider church. Discussing liturgical choices, some clergy felt it was important to offer traditional forms of worship to older Black worshippers, whilst others felt the church should be more innovative. The vast majority of research participants agreed with involving Black worshippers within the liturgy. The idea here was to foster Black leadership role models and empower the congregation by making Black membership visible. This would help to overcome the marginalization felt by Black church members in a White-majority church.

CHAPTER FOUR

BLACK CLERGY DISCONTENT

THE RESEARCH STRATEGY FOR my PhD research was to devise a system of data collection that would provide us with evidence of the existence of a political agenda that was likely to be detrimental to Black Christians in general, and Black clergy in particular. It was hypothesized that it was this agenda that would determine the mode of involvement of Black Christians in the Church of England. The research design consisted of selective interviews that focused upon the Englishness of the Anglican Church and the formation of inner-city policies. By asking questions relevant to the social and political dynamics of the church at that time, I gained access to the subjective perspective of Black clergy as both the recipients and implementers of inner-city policies. The strategy twenty years later is to focus specifically on Black clergy's well-being, or lack of it, within the Church of England and to place this in a post-inner-city context.

The Stephen Lawrence inquiry defined institutional racism as follows:

> The collective failure of an organisation to provide an appropriate and professional service to people because of their colour, culture or ethnic origin. It can be seen or detected in processes, attitudes and behavior which

amount to discrimination through unwitting prejudice, ignorance, thoughtlessness and racist stereotyping which disadvantage minority ethnic people.[1]

The Church of England report, *Present and Participating*,[2] uses this definition to show how the established church in England is institutionally racist. Thus, institutional racial discrimination originates not only in the operation of established and respected values in society, but also in church structures and procedures. To understand the concept of institutionalized racism, we must not only look to the racist belief system which operates in society, but accept the possibility that certain institutions—including churches, through a system of subcultures—are able to amplify these values. Thus, the actions of policymakers and institutional functionaries can have an adverse impact on racial groups, even when race is not mentioned, or when there is no intention to discriminate.

Present and Participating calls upon the Church of England to acknowledge the importance of the inclusion of ethnic minorities in the leadership and decision-making processes of the church. The report recognizes that Asian and Black clergy are marginalized within the Church of England. Minority ethnic clergy are allowed to function only within certain inner-city parishes and are prevented from progressing through the career structure to the higher echelons of the church. This institutional racism goes largely unchallenged as the presence of Asian and Black clergy is not affirmed by the institution. *Present and Participating* responded to this situation by setting out reasons why the involvement of Asian and Black people and their clergy was important for the Church of England. These included the need to accept the diversity that Asian and Black people brought with them. In any event, such diversity was clearly good for a White church that was probably in decline. Thus, if the institution could embrace these diverse minority ethnic worshippers, then the Church of England would be able to reconnect with the worldwide Anglican communion. It is

1. Macpherson, *Report of the Stephen Lawrence Inquiry*, para 6.34.
2. Archbishops' Council, *Present and Participating*.

in this context that minority ethnic Anglicans could be valued for their unique and significant contributions.

Two Church of England reports provide useful background statistics on ethnic diversity. They cover a period of fifteen years, leading to the publication of a comprehensive diversity survey which included the ethnic background of clergy in 2005. They provide us with information about ethnic backgrounds of those in positions of responsibility within the church at both the parish and diocese levels. The focus is church membership and attendance. *How We Stand*[3] is about Black Anglican membership of the Church of England in the 1990s. Black Anglicans were 1 percent of the church's membership and 1.7 percent of Sunday attendance. According to *How We Stand*, the Church of England had ninety-two Black Anglican clergy in parish ministry in 1992. *Called to Act Justly*[4] found 1 percent of stipendiary clergy and 2.1 percent of nonstipendiary clergy came from minority ethnic backgrounds.

The collection of 2002 statistics provided by the Research and Statistics Department of the Archbishops' Council put minority ethnic membership at 3.2 percent. In 2005, the Church of England conducted an audit of the ethnic diversity of its clergy. The General Synod of the Church of England, at its July 2003 sitting, supported the recommendations of *Called to Act Justly*, which called for an audit of the ethnic backgrounds of Anglican clergy. The idea was to find out what proportion of clergy could be classified as belonging to minority ethnic backgrounds and relate this to the offices they held. The audit would establish a baseline that would enable further monitoring of clergy and provide some insight into their demographic background and how this might change over a period of time. They also wanted to know how many Black clergy were British-born. The initial audit was not carried out until 2004. The 2005 Clergy Diversity Audit used the 2001 government census categories to record participants' own perceived ethnic backgrounds. These included White, Mixed (the term "Dual Heritage" is used in this report), Asian or Asian British, Black or Black British, and

---

3. General Synod of the Church of England, *How We Stand,* 43.

4. Archbishops' Council, *Called to Act Justly,* 22.

Chinese or other. 9,921 out of 11,477 Church of England clergy completed and returned their questionnaires. Thus, there was a remarkably high response rate of 86 percent. The findings were as follows: 2.2 percent of all Church of England clergy had self-reported that they were members of an ethnic minority as defined by the 2001 government census. As we would expect, the majority of clergy (97.6 percent) came from White backgrounds. The largest so-called minority ethnic backgrounds for clergy were Black/Black British (0.9 percent) and Dual Heritage (0.7 percent). The audit showed that 23 percent of Black clergy were British-born, with the highest proportions coming from Dual Heritage ethnic groups. Fifty-seven percent of Black Clergy were born outside the UK (26 percent came from Africa, while 23 percent came from Asia). These figures did not include retired clergy who were no longer on the payroll. To put this into a wider context, between 1998 and 2005, Black and Asian attendance increased by 19 percent, while White church attendance decreased by the same percentage.[5]

There are proportionally more people from Black/British ethnic backgrounds among laity than among clergy within the Church of England. The audit also makes comparisons with the national civil population. In the civil population as a whole, 4 percent of people are from Asian/Asian British backgrounds, but less than 1 percent of all clergy come from these backgrounds. Among Church of England clergy, all minority ethnic backgrounds are underrepresented. The diversity audit gave focus to the ethnic background of Anglican Clergy who are in receipt of a stipend, but it does not tell us what positions of responsibility they hold. It is far from clear how many Asian and Black clergy are of incumbent status although the assumption made is that the majority function in a parish or chaplaincy context.

So how does this relate to my contemporary research? How many clergy were interviewed and how were they selected? What was their age, ministerial experience, gender, and status within the church hierarchy? And what of the means by which I went about

5. See Brierley, *Pulling Out of the Nosedive*, 90–92.

identifying and contacting suitable research participants? Like my first sample, the six research participants were drawn from across a diocesan area, and none had any responsibility beyond their parochial remit. However, these were very experienced people who could be compared with their White counterparts who were members of the hierarchy. This was a deliberate strategy on my part as a researcher so that I could later compare like with like. There were three men (Asian, Black South African, and Black English) and three women (Asian, Afro-Caribbean, and Black English). There were no differences in response in terms of gender or ethnicity within these sample groups. However, Black and Asian research participants had things to say about how they perceived the White ethnicity of the Church of England, which distinguishes them from White clergy.

So, what about the research questions? I decided not to run the research again using the same questions. The new research used different questions from the earlier work and with a different sample group. There were two reasons I decided not to go about it in that way. Firstly, the church as a context has changed as had the world context in which it was set. Secondly, I was not entirely convinced that these questions were precise enough at the time, let alone now.

The questions from my PhD research were very broad and open ended, and perhaps, at times, deliberately naive. The research used the inner-city context as a lens for the lived experience of Black clergy and their identity politics. The first four questions ascertained how the clergy perceived the church with regard to what they thought the church was doing, what it should be doing for those who live in the cities and urban areas of deprivation, and in particular the Afro-Caribbean community. They were as follows:

- What is the Church of England doing in the cities and urban areas of deprivation?

- What should the Church of England be doing in the cities and urban areas of deprivation?

- What do you think the Church of England should be doing for those who live in these areas?

- What do you think the Church of England should be doing for the Afro-Caribbean Community?

Twenty years on, the context has changed and so has the lived experience of the Church of England clergy. However, my resolve is not to preempt the findings, but to listen seriously to my research participants. Clearly the questions had to be phrased differently to get insight into the contemporary experience of Black clergy and to find out if things had changed at all since the 1990s. I came to the realization that since our research participants are all experienced members of the Church of England clergy, although not members of its hierarchy, I should ask them direct questions about their situations. Two opening questions replaced the four questions from the research I conductred during the nineties:

- What is the Church of England doing to foster the ministry of Black and Asian Christians?

- What should the Church of England be doing to foster the ministry of Black and Asian Christians?

These questions produced some interesting responses. The majority of the clergy interviewed told me that nothing had been done to foster Black and Asian ministries and that they were not the focus of any program of equality and justice. A typical response was as follows:

Nothing constructive that I am aware of. (RP31)

Some research participants went a lot further and pointed out that the system was too busy looking out for its own. They recognized that, as a marginalized group, they were not on anyone's radar within the hierarchy of the church. The feeling was that Black and Asian clergy were being ignored because those who made the decisions about senior deployment knew only too well that they could not accommodate marginalized groups as well as their White and privileged counterparts. Clearly our research participants know that their needs, if taken seriously, would only be a distraction to the real motivation of the institution. No one was under any illusion as to whether or not senior positions were on promise to White clergy because of their family connections:

> What is the Church of England doing to help Black people in Ministry? Don't make me laugh! They are doing nothing to help the likes of us. Yes, they are trying to manage and control us to be grateful and dependent on their privilege. It is like a race relations industry with a few Uncle Toms to toe their line and keep the lid on things. There may be one Black Archbishop but that has not changed anything for the rest of us, if anything, things have got worse and White privilege rules the day. If Black and Asian people get into ministry in the first place, they have to be better than their White counterparts; when it comes to middle and senior management, we are nowhere to be seen. Twenty years plus down the line, I have applied for those senior jobs that do get advertised and I have waited patiently, with my impressive CV, to be head-hunted for those jobs that do not get to be advertised. But, you know, I could wait till Judgement Day to be called for an interview and appointment. Colleagues, many of whom, actually, are less able than myself, people that I trained with, are now archdeacons, Deans of cathedrals, and even bishops. But where is my three-cornered hat? I am invisible to those people who make the decisions about clergy deployment. As a Black person, you can reach your glass ceiling very quickly. The senior jobs in the church are for the White elites. (RP32)

> If you have a home accent and have been through the British educational system, then you are perceived as a threat, knowing the inside view, as it were. (RP35)

So, what should the church be doing? The just-referenced research participant above suggested:

> the church should look at itself critically and ask what possible rationale it can have to be so excluding. In the early days of immigration in the middle of the last century, most newcomers were deeply religious and had

tremendous loyalty to the church having been members back home. They were rejected time and time again here. The church has never addressed this intellectual disloca- tion concerning exclusivity. The church cannot engage because it refuses to recognize the process that is actually going on. (RP35)

Another interesting reply to my second question was that the church institution should not be targeting Black and Asian clergy for what might be referred to as affirmative action. This was an acknowledgment of a need for a longer-term strategy toward meritocracy:

I don't think the Church of England should be doing anything to foster the ministry of Black and Asian Chris- tians. The church should be genuinely seeking to find the image of God in all Christians and to empower and liberate it. (RP31)

The contemporary research asked two issues on identity politics:

- Can you tell me what aspects of the Church of England enable Black and Asian Christians to identify with it? As a so-called ethnic minority member of the clergy, what do you identify with that gives the church meaning for you?

- The Church of England talks about Black and Asian church attenders as ethnic minority Anglicans. Are you comfortable with this categorization? Does it make you aware of your own ethnic identity? Do you see yourself as an ethnic minority?

Research participants made distinctions between the church, and the context in which they found themselves as a practicing Christian in their mode of identification. Thus, they identified with the Jesus of history and the Christ of faith in the world:

The historical persona of Jesus and the historical marker of Christ with the pulse of the Holy Spirit to survive the potential bitterness of daily exclusion . . . I think the Gospel should make you feel like an alien in whatever culture you are in—whether adopted culture or culture of origin. I do often feel that I am among enemies at certain church events where senior clergy are together. I think our identity as Christians should transcend and transform human connectedness as we become invited to be direct agents of the Kingdom. (RP31)

What do I identify with? Only Jesus, but his church leaves a lot to be desired. (RP35)

Four of the six research participants were not happy with the prevailing concept of multiculturalism. They did not feel it was an adequate term to emphasize the importance of diversity:

I believe in diversity. I am sick of this multi shit. Diversity must be respected. When "different" is used, that is a diminishing word. I always ask where people come from in order to give respect, to gain some understanding, tune myself in to them. I need to know even locally, from which part of the city. Everyone's "ethnic," damn it. There's just so much bullshit. You can't even put Pakistanis and Indians together after 60 years of separation. Making connections and valuing people, that's pastoral care. (RP34)

Only one research participant was comfortable with the term "ethnic minority" and thought there was a political advantage in using it:

Sometimes it can be an advantage, being an ethnic minority, in getting grants, but this can also be a double-edged sword because you are viewed differently. Am I comfortable with categorization? Yes, in the sense that it makes it clear there is a difference. If we were all the same, then Black and Asian issues would not be dealt with. If there are issues, it is better to be identified in a group. The concept of ethnic is too wide—it needs to be refined. What does it mean to be an ethnic minority anyway? What other minorities or disabilities are there? (RP33)

The majority of research participants disliked this term and felt marginalized by its use. They expressed a number of concerns as to how it has been deployed by the church:

> I see the term "ethnic minority" as pejorative because it is based on the assumptions of White people. "Minority ethnic" is okay so long as you are using it as descriptor of a particular demographic. It should not be used to identify people to be marginalized. You know, like someone coming into a chapter meeting and announcing, "A load of poufters are now coming to my church . . ." That makes it even more painful to hear members of BME being disparaging of and rejecting women and gay people. After all, there are no willies in heaven. (RP35)

The contemporary research questions had to consider exceptions to the rule with the preferment of John Sentamu as the Archbishop of York. The questions also had to ask: If this is a concession, will it be the only one for many years to come? When I prepared for this research, I realized it would seem very personal to be asking questions about a particular prominent bishop in the Church of England. As I make sense of research participants' responses to questions, there are two things to say here. Firstly, it shows a lack of Black leadership that there is only one Black bishop to refer to, so it would be pointless seeking anonymity for him. Secondly, when people take up public office, to some extent they become public property. In asking questions about John Sentamu's leadership we are talking about him as an officeholder with considerable responsibility within the institutional life of the Church of England. My comments are restricted to his role and function, and do not extend to him in his person.

So, was John Sentamu subject to discriminatory practices when another candidate for the Canterbury post with limited experience as a bishop was appointed? Thus, my questions here were as follows:

- John Sentamu has been described by the media as a self-publicist and an autocrat. Are you aware of other potential candidates for the post of Archbishop of Canterbury being talked about in these terms?

- Since John Sentamu became the first Black Archbishop of York, what effect has his appointment had upon the advancement of other Black clergy to senior positions of responsibility in the Church of England? To your knowledge, can you please tell me how Archbishop John has supported equality in the appointment of Black and Women clergy?

Research participants felt that bishop Sentamu had received bad press and that there was no evidence that his style of leadership was any more autocratic than that of other senior bishops being considered for the post at Canterbury:

> Local knowledge refers to Richard Charters as a bully and autocrat, but this is not cited in the national and international press. In fact, to my understanding Charters has more frequently been referred to as statesman-like. I question where these boundaries lie, particularly since the successful candidate comes from the same voracious plutocracy as Charters. (RP31)

> The bishop of London did not get a good press either even though it is known he does not support ethnic minorities. The bad press Sentamu was subjected to was racist. Clearly he does not have a monopoly on autocracy as a style of leadership. As a publicist, this is not a strength for Sentamu because he is Black. (RP33)

Research participants were clear that Sentamu did not appoint Black people to positions of authority in the York Diocese or anywhere else in the Church of England. They felt that this was his decision and not something imposed by White colleagues. There was also an interesting gender dimension here with Sentamu being perceived by one research participant as positive about women's ministry:

> On women clergy he is very good, that is White women clergy. As for promoting Black people of either gender, I cannot think of anyone. In York Province, he is the only

senior Black person. I know experienced and able Black clergy in that province who could have been appointed to senior posts. I don't think I have any good things to say about Sentamu. I don't think he is being stopped by White people he just has not appointed Black people to senior posts. (RP33)

More typical responses which made no gender distinction were as follows:

None—yet. I get a Christmas and an Easter card from him every year and I was invited to his enthronement. I used to greet him with a hug, but when I saw him standing alone for a moment and went up to hug him, he flinched away which told me a lot. I don't follow matters in York, but I am sure that if he had been promoting BME and women, it would have found its way into the media. (RP35)

I am not aware of Archbishop John doing anything in support of equality where appointments are concerned. He likes to appoint White people as archdeacons and to other such posts even when it is known there are more suitable candidates who happen to be Black. (RP32)

So far as I know, Archbishop John has offered no support. (RP34)

Discontent and frustration were expressed about this situation and one of the research participants went as far as to say that they were glad that Sentamu did not become the next Archbishop of Canterbury given his record on Black clergy appointments:

Sentamu, on account of his appalling record for promoting Black clergy, didn't deserve Canterbury and I am glad he didn't get it. (RP32)

Clearly, if Sentamu had been active in promoting other Black clergy, then competition for York and Canterbury may well have included some of those able-but-forgotten clergy.

So why has so much been invested in the leadership of John Sentamu as a change agent rather than an establishment figure?

Clearly there was an expectation, as the only Black bishop, that he would nurture the ministry of other Black people within the church, given the inequality that is to be found within the institution. So, was the appointment of a Black male as the second most senior bishop in the Church of England an answer to the equality issue or a significant part of the problem? In other words, was Archbishop Sentamu's appointment about genuine liberation and change or part of a negative process that would prevent other Black clergy from realizing their potential for leadership? So how do we depersonalize and explain the behavior of marginalized individuals who attain high office? One research participant wondered if Sentamu was himself a victim and experiencing "capture bonding" as characterized by the Stockholm Syndrome. Stockholm Syndrome (also known as terror-bonding or trauma bonding) originated as a concept from a hostage situation in Sweden in 1973 when bank employees, following their six-day ordeal, started to identify with their captors.[6] The idea here is that, as a Black person, Sentamu had identified not with other Black people, but with White privilege, which is in contradiction to the interests of the constituent group from which he originates:

> I have read a number of blogs that would suggest that Sentamu, like a lot of Black people when they get a position of influence, start to identify with our oppressors and not their own people. It is just like when people are held as hostages, some of them start to identify with their captors. I think they call it Stockholm Syndrome. (RP32)

This is an interesting idea, but what does the research actually tell us? There is no evidence from my findings to show that Black leadership had been taken hostage by the institution of the Church of England. Research participants did not perceive the one Black bishop as a captive with false identifications. However, research participants had no difficulty in calling to account the leadership of John Sentamu because he had failed to appoint Black clergy to senior posts. As far as research participants were concerned,

6. See Mackenzie, "Stockholm Syndrome Revisited." See also Huddleston-Muttai, "Sambo Mentality and the Stockholm Syndrome," 344–57.

Sentamu was making his own decisions about appointments. That the system could trust him to do so in such a way as not to challenge the existing structure of privilege which limits Black leadership does not make this a case of Stockholm Syndrome. What we call it as a phenomenon still vexes me.

Perhaps the most helpful explanation is to acknowledge that senior officeholders may well talk about liberation and equality issues, but rarely implement such change within the system they have responsibility for. Why should John Sentamu be any different from other bishops in the Church of England?

Research participants were asked the following questions with regard to the appointment of Justin Welby as the Archbishop of Canterbury: Justin Welby was appointed as Archbishop of Canterbury and not John Sentamu. What do you think were the major factors that informed this decision? How will this affect the appointments procedures and outcome for Black clergy seeking high office?

The majority of research participants felt that Sentamu had been over looked and that there had been a racialized aspect to the appointment procedure. Only one research participant was willing to give the institution the benefit of the doubt.

> I really don't know, I don't think you can read anything into it, there have been plenty of other examples of York not automatically leading to Canterbury. I have no axe to grind, no contribution to make. Maybe Welby is the right person. (RP34)

Typical responses to this question were:

> The appointment procedure is covered in mystery. When they elected a new Pope, we knew who the cardinals were, and they could be approached. It remains to be seen if Welby would be a good Archbishop. I am not really interested in the man because of his level of experience in the church. I don't know how this decision was made. A lot has been said about his skills as a reconciler. I don't see it. (RP33)

I don't know what the procedures were for this appointment. I think there is some kind of commission. I certainly was not asked what I thought nor were any of my parishioners. If you join a political party you get a say in who is to be the leader but in the Church of England it is all behind closed doors, and only the rich and privileged are consulted. (RP32)

We have got one Black foreign-born Archbishop whose existence is apparently so repellent that a campaign was launched to block his appointment. The Eton-educated son of a White conman who has not been a bishop a year has been translated to Canterbury amongst vocabulary against Sentamu that does not seek to cloak its racism. The same things could have been said about Richard Charters regarding arrogance and autocratic style, but he is a White man and well-connected within the Establishment, so it has not been said . . . Welby as the result of anybody-apart-from-Sentamu lobby. The pattern for future discrimination is clear, especially since at the moment of this discussion, very little is known about Welby. (RP31)

According to research participants, the situation with regard to future appointments of Black clergy to senior posts had not been changed by the Canterbury appointment. Furthermore, they were not convinced that a Black Archbishop would make much of a difference unless that person was serious about appointing other Black bishops and Black middle managers. As for the new Archbishop, clearly he was not everyone's favorite and comparisons were implied with other contenders for this post. Justin Welby's translation was seen as a privileged appointment, making the Church of England look self-satisfied and its leadership exposed as well heeled and well connected.

The following summarizes the feeling of Black clergy toward the white leadership of the Church of England:

Of course, Welby is massively better qualified at being a bishop. He has worked in ordinary poor parishes, he is of humble origins and has risen through the ranks through his own endeavours. Despite being at an ordinary comprehensive school, his towering intellect meant he got a good degree against the odds. Really understandable—from the inside. This is a man who couldn't speak French, yet he worked for a French oil company, a post obtained through a well-connected relative. His wife has spoken of coping with the change from a salary of £100k to one of £10k when Welby took his first post as a curate. She says she learnt to do things with chicken livers. As if they did not have a house worth a fortune, and surely they must have saved on such a lavish income. It's all lies. Does she think anyone is fooled? Welby has never really done anything, seen anything through. So, who has rocketed him up? He is supposed to be skilled at conflict resolution, but he has already said that he cannot resolve conflict within the church. (RP35)

Despite significant changes in the mode of expression of xenophobia and racist intolerance, the Church of England remains a highly discriminatory institution. Thus, this reality and its consequences for Black Anglicans remain the context within which we must do our theology concerning Black clergy deployment. The theology is political because it is the Black God-talk of Black marginalized clergy.

I attended the Black Anglican Celebration for the Decade of Evangelism held at York in July 1994. I have referred to this event as an example of "good samboism" whereby Black participants plead to be allowed to join the White membership club of the Church of England on receipt of a good sense of rhythm.[7] To me, that was the message of the conference, not conscientization. I have sought ever since to challenge such sinfully naive enthusiasm which amounts to acquiescing to your own exploitation.

The Church of England's response to the presence of black people, both in society and in the church itself, is from within a race relations problematic. This approach is concerned with the characteristics, attitudes, and actions of those who are defined as belonging to various races and the harmony or lack of tension

7. Isiorho, "Black Theology in Urban Shadow," 29–48.

between them. The focus is upon the Black worshippers themselves insofar as this will allow the institution to ask why more Black people don't belong to the Church of England, while at the same time promoting the pluralistic integration of those who do. This problematic does not ask questions about racism, radicalized relations, or the attitudes, actions, and motivations of White worshippers within the institution of the Church of England. Furthermore, this problematic inhibits the assessment process of the relative impact of multiple variables that are involved in the racialization process that introduce meaning to previously racially unclassified relationships, practices, or groups.

The emergence of the Black majority church can be found in the immigrant-host relationships of the 1950s and the development of a race relations problematic which called upon people of Afro-Caribbean and Asian descent to assimilate with the host culture of British society. A development of this paradigm was pluralism, which posits that Black and Asian people be left to form their own distinct groups, at least initially, within the host culture, with a view to eventual integration, if not complete assimilation, at a later date. This was said to be a way of celebrating diversity, but was really an effective, though subtle, marker of difference. Pluralism answers the apparent neglect of the culturally significant contributions of the marginalized that assimilation would seek by definition to deny. Thus, either by way of assimilation or by pluralism, equilibrium is restored to the benefit of the host culture. While assimilation denies the identity of Black and Asian people, pluralism denies the citizenship of the indigenous non-White population. Both models have the effect of preventing Black and Asian people from acting in their own social and economic interests. Assimilationists advocated that immigrants should learn to fit in by adapting to the values and expectations associated with the British way of life. Look at the current issue around the desire of the government that all newcomers to this country should be able to speak English. By emphasizing this one-way process of adaptation, these assimilationists found themselves neglecting the cultural contributions of what they perceived to be the other. Pluralists, on the other hand, encouraged the maintenance of distinct ethnic cultural identities in an attempt to integrate everyone, including the British born children of immigrants.

It can be argued that the ideas of integration, even if naive, are, at face value, laudable enough. However, the real problem for Black theology has to be integration of whom and into what. Integration with White society could well mean the incorporation of Black and Asian people into a system of power strengthened by racism, patriarchy, and wider inequalities. Clearly the idea of cultural diversity is very different from the European notions of assumed normality, and the subsequent superiority, of White traditions.

This chapter is premised upon the idea that if the norm is White, then Black people and their Black clergy are beyond the norm and therefore are not part of the big society of modern conservativism. This contemporary norm is clearly White. I am suggesting here that the big society ethos contributes to a process that utilizes Western thought and language to mark out who belongs and who does not. This big society presumes a cohesiveness which excludes Black voices since it depends on an historical perspective which draws upon White identity and White institutions like the Church of England. The African and Asian diaspora is unlikely to have the same response to group memory of the bulldog spirit of Dunkirk even though Black people have inhabited these islands from Elizabethan times.

The big society, like the Church of England, is a signifier of Englishness. It is a white and privileged phenomenon and as such should be critiqued by the common good and the concept of the social gospel with its bias to the poor. It is post-multicultural, and it relies upon an historical perspective that gives focus to the idea that the natural inhabitants of the UK are White. The single British identity inherited from "New Labour" is superseded by a national cohesiveness which is both English and White, so questions about Englishness are also questions about Whiteness as a cultural construct—the norm turning anything connected with Black into a category of dependence.

Whiteness, therefore, has no consciousness of its own and exists appositionally to others. In this way, the notion of Englishness is used to signify privilege and turns Black people and their Black clergy into outsiders. Because cultural whiteness is the norm, White people are under no pressure of any sort to conform; they are already a significant group. There are no explanations to be made either to themselves or to anyone else.

This entangles the White mindset into some confusion with ideas of contradiction and splintering. Englishness does not enjoy the same privileges as Whiteness, so the more closely it is tied to Whiteness the fewer questions it must answer. The gently ironic nostalgia, perpetuated by writers such as John Bjetman in "Westminster Abbey" and many other poems, portray this, despite this irony being missed by so many White readers. Imaginary but persuasive drama and other narratives show how the English represent themselves to themselves.

There was considerable concern amongst our research participants that Sentamu had not appointed Black clergy to positions of responsibility. I explored the Stockholm Syndrome as an explanation for this and found it lacking as, wrenched from its original context, it has little to offer in application to this research. I am also aware that as a theoretical model it is easily falsified by the example of the few senior officeholders from humble origins who have clearly not been taken hostage by the system.

Someone who could have claimed great fame and wealth but who has remained humbly walking with his God is Desmond Tutu. In 2012, writing in *The Observer* newspaper, Desmond Tutu explained why he had pulled out of a conference on leadership because he could not share a platform with Tony Blair. Tutu reminds us all that the current and potentially catastrophic destabilization in the world was brought about by the direct and unfounded actions of the then-American administration, supported by Tony Blair. What is frightening is how avowedly Christian men— George W. Bush and Blair—can go to war and not be called to account, scorning the many millions of us who demonstrated our feelings of disapproval. Despite a lack of evidence as to the reality of the weapons of mass destruction—I thought we in the West had those!—against a groundswell of popular opposition, Bush and Blair hurled us into wars that continue to cause suffering of Holocaust-level proportions, a toxic combination of the interests of capital, oil, and White power against the rest of the world. Yet Tutu was able to challenge this with profoundly humbling love. What a prayerful and Christlike demonstration to us all about how to take our leaders to task and affirm their humanity in an embracing and inclusive manner.

The Holy Spirit empowers those of us of faith to become the physical presence of Jesus in the middle of this beautiful and tormented world. In his body, Jesus is in heaven, but, in his Spirit, he is here on earth and active, moving us to be his agents, healers, reconcilers, prophets, martyrs, and downright irritants to systems grown fat and complacent on exploitation, injustice, division, and exclusion. May his light, life, and love inspire us to work for reconciliation, peace, comfort, freedom, and equality.

CONCLUSION

BLACK CLERGY WELL-BEING

Some Conclusions on Employment Practices in the Church of England

JUST AS I AM about to leave my present diocese, a new bishop has arrived saying he intends to give focus to work with children and young people. This is not very original and gives little encouragement to what is essentially a rural diocese. Money and resources will be found for short-term pioneering projects giving focus to youth work in the few towns and cities. The new bishop could have said he wanted to focus on the homeless and destitute and that he wanted to equip clergy and lay leaders to do the same. There is plenty of opportunity for that work in the urban areas as well as the countryside. It would be interesting if I could find an example of a senior leader in the Church of England who wanted to encourage ministry among the elderly and dying even though this group represents the majority of the faithful in our churches. I have come across clergy who refuse to consider working in a parish without youth projects and many young people. Sadly, parishes with lots of older people are the rubbish end of ministry. Please don't misunderstand me. There is nothing wrong with working with young people, but it is not the only aspect of ministry and should not be at the expense of everything else that happens at church.

We hear a lot about mission-shaped churches, fresh expressions of church, and how these relate to work with young people. My argument is that fresh expressions are not a school of thought, but rather a modus operandi which links into nothing at all. If it were a school of thought, it would involve a central philosophy which could be communicable, explained, and challenged. As a modus operandi, fresh expressions are just a way of doing things within the church—a set of pragmatics without theological justification. The Christian church worldwide is not failing, so why does it now need fresh expressions? A third of the world's population is Christian. What is not working is the Eurocentric view of church and its dependence upon global capitalism.

So, what can we say about contemporary employment practices in the Church of England, particularly with reference to the well-being of Black clergy? During the first part of this book I have talked about my own experience as a Black clergyperson in the Church of England. Clearly, the underrepresentation of Black clergy in senior positions is the context in which I write. However, *Mission, Anguish, and Defiance* did not set out to prove this disproportionality since it is widely acknowledged within the literature of the church's own publications. Furthermore, the theoretical assumption on which the book is based, namely that Black clergy underrepresentation is the product of institutional racism in the Church of England, is also documented elsewhere. *Mission Anguish and Defiance* is not about how many Black bishops and archdeacons there are in the Church of England, although it has been noted that senior Black officeholders are few and all of these are foreign born. The focus of this book has been the lived experiences of Black clergy whose deployment has been in the Church of England. Clearly, Black clergy are overlooked when it comes to preferment to positions of greater responsibility. The appointment of one Black archbishop may have broken the glass ceiling for one individual, but what if the York appointment remains an isolated case, as looks increasingly likely?

I was at an ecumenical gathering a few years ago when it was seriously suggested that Black Anglicans should leave the Church of England and form their own church. After all, is this not what John Wesley did? If that were to happen, there would be very small White congregations left in most of our cities and large urban areas. The Black churches are growing in all denominations at a time when White churches are declining and, in some cases, closing down.

My testimony demonstrates that, within a few years of ordination, I reached the glass ceiling preventing any progression within the structure of the Church of England. My aspirations for a cathedral ministry in chapter two demonstrate this very clearly. In 1998, I completed my PhD on the mode of involvement of Black Christians in the Church of England, with special reference to English ethnicity. Twenty years later, I wanted to know if there have been any significant changes in the deployment of Black clergy and their well-being. This book explores the outcomes from interviews with a sample group of Black clergy, attempting to make explicit the participants' sense of inclusion/exclusion within the Church of England, thereby identifying dominant themes and offering some interpretations of their experiences within the church. Alongside this, we look at an agenda about English ethnicity as the driving force for Black involvement in the Church of England, giving focus to research participants' understanding of their sense of well-being within this institution.

Responses from research participants in this book are often in the style of rhetoric and polemic, directed at the Church of England hierarchy as regards its marginalizing and excluding of Black clergy from its higher ranks. However, this is a serious piece of social and political research and should not be confused with journalism because of the colloquial and anecdotal nature of some of the responses. The subjective character of research participants' contributions demonstrates a righteous indignation, a perfectly intelligent emotional response to the perceived injustices of clergy deployment within the established church.

Englishness seems to be the core image of the Church of England. This comes with the typically English approach of saying the polite thing. Is it this that drives the church to make public protestations that it wants to see an increase in the involvement of Black people at all levels? It is almost as if the church is saying things it does not truly mean as we can see the system has not been radically changed in order to effect that inclusion. So, we are left with questions about how serious the church is if it will not bring about the institutional changes necessary to implement its stated policies. The church continues to render Black clergy invisible and undetectable, as it does with many women clergy.

From my research during the 1990s, there came an almost overwhelming sense of neglect and abandonment. I used the image of a child sent to the corner in the nursery, denied the food the others are having, then being forgotten and left alone. There was a sense that the church was being run like a club from which our research participants were being deliberately excluded. This is what led to the questions that the Black clergy would like to put to the bishops. These questions were a protest against the lack of kingdom-effective action on the part of senior office holders. The feeling of being punished for some unknown and unknowable offense was deep; not alienation, but exclusion and subjugation. What we are looking at, therefore, is a type of pain that is damaging at many levels and will have long-term effects not, of course, merely on those who are the primary victims, but also spiritually on the church itself.

Although our bishops are aware that there is discontent among Black clergy, they continue to focus on issues surrounding lay involvement or dealing with matters elsewhere on the planet. There is doublespeak going on as the bishops express the desire to appoint Black clergy to posts of significant responsibility, whilst they murmur about the snare of tokenism. Given this, we can only conclude that the church has no regard for the talents and long experience of the clergy in our sample. Are we to conclude that they really do not care, that the suffering is insignificant to them? That leads to all sorts of possible conclusions about a church based on the two dominical commandments to love both God and your neighbor.

In order to move closer to a measure of meritocracy in the Church of England, we need more opportunities for Black clergy to take up middle management positions such as archdeacons, residential canons, and cathedral deans. Future Black bishops, both male and female, could be called from this group. At present, there is no shortage of able Black and Asian clergy to fill these posts, the problem is the willingness of the system to deploy them.

The church has, for far too long, made its senior appointments on the basis of who you know and not what you know. These issues have to be addressed by the whole church. We hold a mirror up to society, yes, but, in our turn, we must act as a model to society. How can the church be serious about its place in the world, seeking to change the lives of ordinary people, if its institution does not conform to the principles of the kingdom? This, of course, is an ideal and many of our research participants doubt the sincerity of the church at an institutional level to do any of these things.

Staying with the notion of "ideal" for a little longer, what needs to happen for Black clergy to respond in positive terms about their well-being? The White institution of the Church of England will have to learn to give us the space which would allow Black people and their clergy to be there as fellow inheritors of the kingdom, rather than some ethnic minority. The church must accept that this could well mean that some White people do not get the positions they think should be theirs. They even expect to take these positions when the post is about Black advocacy. Until recently the Church of England employed a White man as the National Training Coordinator for its Centre for Black Leadership. How seriously can you take that? This is not the first time that the Church of England has shot itself in the foot with an inappropriate appointment. White people have taken up similar posts as diocesan officers and even as national advisers at Church House, Westminster.

We live in a finite world with limited resources but, if we are serious about freeing people to do those good works set for them, then some White people will have to step aside so that others can take leadership roles. That means a sacrificial dedication to racial justice. We need to understand that we are light years away from a meritocracy. To effect change at the grassroots level in the parochial and synodical structures of the Church of England, change has to be seen at all levels of ministry, particularly at the top. Black clergy are not asking for a share in an unjust system, but rather they want to see a reform of the system for the common good.

So what needs to be done? To begin with, the church hierarchy must be on board for this justice development work. When I say, on board, I mean truly so—not merely paying lip service. The Church of England should seek to establish a greater connection between what bishops say about racial justice issues and what they actually do to advance such policies. The Church of England should demonstrate its willingness to do this by including a serious consideration of the needs of Asian and Black clergy whenever reorganization of financial and human resources takes place. The next round of fresh expressions, or its successor, must involve so-called minority ethnic Anglicans. We need to demonstrate the relevance of Christ's liberating message for all people. Thus, whilst facing the church we must develop that conversation, we must also, whilst facing the world, show that racial justice is being done. It is also about the world-facing problems of all Christians seeking to realize their faith as the kingdom of God.

So how should I conclude this book? And what are the signposts for further research? It would seem that the position of Black clergy is just as marginalized as it was in 2003, and that the appointment of one African-born archbishop has not in any serious way changed the ecclesiastical landscape. It is not my argument that the church is asleep and that somehow a prophetic voice will wake it up; no, rather that the Church of England is pretending to be asleep. This brings the inevitable realization that you cannot wake up someone who is shamming. Clearly this is the time for straight talking, and senior officeholders can choose to listen or not, but let's not pretend that this is a minor problem premised by a few misunderstandings that can be sorted out by race relations and good communication skills.

What of the Church of England's collective failure as an institution to engage justly with its own clergy because of their color, culture, or ethnic origin? And how is this indicated in the church's processes, attitudes, and behaviors? The institutional racism of the Church of England can take the form of a modern version of the biblical parable of the rich man and Lazarus. Like the rich man, the church is not deliberately cruel to Black clergy but, like Lazarus, we are just not on anyone's radar. For the rich man, Lazarus is so insignificant that he functionally does not exist as a person with feelings in his own right. The marginalized clergy of the Church of England are selling the *Big Issue* outside the bishop's palace, but the establishment does not acknowledge their presence. This type of institutional racism disadvantages minority ethnic Anglican clergy through a process of unwitting prejudice. However, this is not the only type of racism within the institution of the church. Another type of racism involves senior officeholders, such as bishops and archdeacons, failing to challenge individual instances of racism on the part of their subordinates, and then seeking to blame prejudice and discriminatory outcomes entirely on the institution and not their own code of conduct.

The Church of England is a bastion of the establishment and yet calls for radical action to combat racism and poverty. The two aspects are not compatible. Thus, the church presents a patronizing and distant persona to the vulnerable urban populace and will not change without prophetic and radical self-examination to the point of self-confrontation. I hope that through this book I have made my own contribution to that process.

It is fashionable to talk about clergy well-being and I have referred to this concept already in this conclusion. However, this would be an abstract starting point for this subject implying positive outcomes. When the context is Black clergy deployment, a more realized term is "clergy discontent" because it comes out of the lived experience of Black people's ministry. We can evaluate the extent of unfulfillment of those vocations in a white majority church like the Church of England. So, any talk of our well-being becomes an apophatic concept for those who feel it, because they know it. And we do all this with one arm tied behind our back, but always in our Lord's glad service. Amen.

BIBLIOGRAPHY

Archbishops' Council. *Called to Act Justly: A Challenge to Include Minority Ethnic People in the Life of the Church of England.* London: Church House, 2003.

———. *Mission-shaped Church: Church Planting and Fresh Expressions of Church in a Changing Context.* London: Church House, 2004.

———. *Present and Participating: A Place at the Table.* London: General Synod of the Church of England, July 2006.

Atkins, Martyn. "What is the Essence of Church?" In *Mission-shaped Questions: Defining Issues for Today's Church,* edited by Steven Croft, 16–28. London: Church House, 2008.

Barley, Lynda. "Can Fresh Expressions of Church Make a Difference?" In *Mission-shaped Questions: Defining Issues for Today's Church,* edited by Steven Croft, 161–72. London: Church House, 2008.

Barton, Mukti. *Freedom is for Freeing: 12 years' (1998–2010) Work as Bishop's Adviser for Black & Asian Ministries.* London: Rougham, 2011.

Brierley, Peter. *The Tide is Running Out: What the English Church Attendance Survey Reveals.* London: Christian Research, 2000.

———. *Pulling Out of the Nosedive—A Contemporary Picture of Churchgoing: What the 2005 English Church Census Reveals.* London: Christian Research, 2006.

Croft, Steven. "Fresh Expressions in a Mixed Economy Church: A Perspective." In *Mission-shaped Questions: Defining Issues for Today's Church,* edited by Steven Croft, 1–15. London: Church House, 2008.

Davison, Andrew, and Alison Milbank. *For the Parish: A Critique of Fresh Expressions.* London: SCM, 2010.

Faith in the City: The Report of the Archbishop's Commission on Urban Priority Areas. London: Church House, 1985.

General Synod of the Church of England. *Called to Lead: A Challenge to Include Minority Ethnic People.* London: Church House, 2000.

———. *HIND Report on Theological Education.* London: Church House, 2003.

———. *How We Stand: A Report on Black Anglican Membership of the Church of England in the 1990s.* London: Church House, 1994.

————*Presence and Engagement: The Churches' Task in a Multi-faith Society.* Atlanta: Scholars, 2005.

Grant, Jacquelyn. *White Women's Christ and Black Women's Jesus: Feminist Christology and Womanist Response.* Atlanta: Scholars, 1989.

Huddleston-Muttai, Barbara A. "The Sambo Mentality and the Stockholm Syndrome Revisited: Another Dimension to an Examination of the Plight of the African American." *Journal of Black Studies* 23.3 (1993) 344–57.

Hull, John. "Mission-shaped and Kingdom Focused?" In *Mission-shaped Questions: Defining Issues for Today's Church,* edited by Stephen Croft, 114–32. London: Church House, 2008

————. *Mission-shaped Church: A Theological Response.* London: CMS, 2006.

Isiorho, David. "Black Clergy Discontent: Selected Interviews on Racialised Exclusion." *Journal of Contemporary Religion* 18.2 (2003) 213–26.

————. "Black Theology, Englishness and the Church of England." In *Postcolonial Black British Theology,* edited by Michael N. Jagessar and Anthony G. Reddie, 62–72. Peterborough, UK: Epworth, 2007.

————. "Black Theology in Urban Shadow." *Black Theology* 1.1 (2002) 29–48.

————. "A Tale of Two Cities: Implicit Assumptions and Mission Strategies in Black and White Majority Churches." *Black Theology* 10.2 (2012) 195–211.

Mackenzie, Ian K. "The Stockholm Syndrome Revisited." *Journal of Police Crisis Negotiations* 4.1 (2004) 5–21.

Macpherson, William. *Report of the Stephen Lawrence Inquiry.* The Stationery Office, February 1999 Cm 4262.

Tilby, Angela. "What Questions Does Catholic Ecclesiology Pose for Contemporary Mission and Fresh Expressions?" In *Mission-shaped Questions: Defining Issues for Today's Church,* edited by Stephen Croft, 78–89. London: Church House, 2008.

Wilkinson, John. *Church in Black and White: The Black Christian Tradition in Mainstream Churches in England: A White Response and Testimony.* Edinburgh: Saint Andrew, 1993.